MONOPOLY
ON SALVATION?

MONOPOLY
ON SALVATION?

*A Feminist Approach
to Religious Pluralism*

Jeannine Hill Fletcher

continuum

NEW YORK • LONDON

2005

The Continuum International Publishing Group Inc
15 East 26 Street, New York, NY 10010

The Continuum International Publishing Group Ltd
The Tower Building, 11 York Road, London SE1 7NX

www.continuumbooks.com

Portions of this text were previously published in "Shifting Identity: The Contribution of Feminist Thought to Theologies of Religious Pluralism," *Journal of Feminist Studies in Religion* 19, no. 2 (Fall 2003): 5–24.

Printed in the United States of America

Library of Congress Cataloging-in-Publication Data

Fletcher, Jeannine Hill.
    Monopoly on salvation? : a feminist approach to religious pluralism / by Jeannine Hill Fletcher.
      p. cm.
    Includes bibliographical references and index.
    ISBN 0-8264-1722-1 (hardcover : alk. paper) –
    ISBN 0-8264-1723-X (pbk. : alk. paper)
    1. Christianity and other religions. 2. Religious pluralism – Christianity. 3. Feminist theology. I. Title.
    BR127.F58 2005
    261.2 – dc22

                                  2005003261

CONTENTS

For Michael

PREFACE

IN 1609, the Christian missionary Roberto de Nobili wrote from India to his Jesuit companions in Rome about an encounter with the leader of a local Hindu community. After a public debate and heated exchange between these two representatives of their respective religious traditions, the learned Brahmin asks his fellow Hindus, "Has this man alone the monopoly on salvation?" One gets the sense that de Nobili's own answer might have been...YES! His faith perspective encouraged an absolute stance that excluded alternative religions from providing the ultimate in human fulfillment. But de Nobili's Hindu companion challenged him to consider the diversity of faiths in a different light.

Today, the encounter of persons from different faith traditions repeats across the globe. The interconnected systems of economics, politics and migration have created even more locations where people of different faiths might meet. Yet, the universal claims of church, temple, mosque and synagogue continue to create passionate allegiances that divide people from one another. Religion often serves as a fuel for ethnic and racial conflicts, engendering violent antagonism among members of the same family, dwellers in the same neighborhood, and citizens of the same country. As globalization rapidly transformed the twentieth century, theologians attempted to address the need for understanding by offering responses to religious difference consistent with Christian belief. While many encouraged a move away from a "monopoly on salvation," they often failed in their ability to provide explanations of religious diversity that valued the distinctiveness of particular traditions. Instead, the "other" was appreciated essentially for how much "like" the Christian he or she was. When theologians did offer a response that insisted on recognizing the differences, it was often to the extreme, creating a portrait of other traditions as so unlike Christianity that conversation and understanding was virtually impossible. At the close of the twentieth century, Christian theology continued to view religious difference as a problem to be overcome — either by erasing it through an imagined sameness or distancing it altogether. At the opening of the twenty-first century, perhaps there is room to see the differences among the religious traditions of the world also in a new light.

The task of this book is to investigate whether a Christian faith perspective can relinquish its "monopoly on salvation" while remaining faithful to the tradition. It simultaneously asks the question of how the distinctiveness of Christianity *and* the distinctiveness of diverse traditions can be honored. As a foundation for the project, chapter 1 will mine the treasures of the tradition to discover how they might orient Christians to the overwhelming evidences of religious difference in the world. Rooted in the concept of God's incomprehensibility as overabundance, the theological foundation is set for seeing the religious differences in the world in a positive light. But the tradition also offers a wealth of active witness in concrete examples of how Christians in the past have tried to engage people of other religious and spiritual traditions. Complementing the theological exploration, chapter 2 provides a reexamination of history to highlight examples of how Christians have crossed religious boundaries in the past. Seen not only through Christian eyes, but through the eyes of persons of other faiths, this exploration of ancient and recent history unearths patterns of encounter for contemporary Christians to consider.

History and classical theology provide the impetus, encouragement and precedent for the dialogue with people of diverse faiths. But the resources of the past are useful only insofar as they continue to speak to the experiences of today. Recognizing this, many Christian theologians have attempted to reconfigure these resources so that they might be relevant for the concerns of contemporary people. In the last half of the twentieth century especially, these projects have been abundant, each attempting in its own way to balance the claims of the Christian tradition with an understanding of people of diverse faiths. A look at the spectrum of these theologies in chapter 3 invites the reader to consider patterns of thought that might frame current interreligious encounters.

While these recent theologies are important for providing a variety of stances toward religious diversity consistent with Christian faith, they do not bring us far enough in the appreciation of difference. That is, difference remains a problem to be explained (and often explained away) rather than a resource for mutual enrichment and theological exploration. One reason that religious difference has not served a positive function in these theologies is that the Christian tradition itself was assumed to be unaffected by those outside its boundaries. But as history shows, Christian self-understanding has often emerged out of the conversation and exchange with persons of different faiths. Encouraged by these precedents, Christians today might also engage across religious boundaries and become affected by persons of other faiths. A feminist analysis of human identity as multifaceted and intrinsically hybrid provides a framework for structuring an engagement across different religious visions that can be mutually enriching. The discussion of such a feminist rethinking of Christian identity is the focus of chapter 4.

Enriched by the engagement with people of other faiths, interreligious dialogue encourages each partner in the conversation to examine more fully their tradition of origin. Christians return to the heart of their own tradition to understand anew the claims and concerns rooted in the New Testament. The final chapter of this book revisits the story of the New Testament and reads it through the lens of interreligious encounter. The culmination is a theology modeled on the life, practice and witness of Jesus of Nazareth that is open to the many patterns of diverse religions as gifts for an encounter with the incomprehensible mystery of God.

The theology of this book emerges from the experience of encounter with friends and colleagues of diverse faiths. I am grateful to each as they have, in countless ways, helped me to develop my Christian theological perspective.

This book also has developed under the guidance and friendship of an invaluable mentor. There are very few ways to say thank you to someone who has transformed my life in the way Francis Schüssler Fiorenza has. Not one word of this book could have been written without his influence and untiring encouragement. He has my deepest gratitude for all he has done to challenge my thinking, clarify my arguments and celebrate my successes.

I was fortunate to have the gift of additional theologians who guided my graduate work and deeply influenced the thinking that produced this book. I hope that Gordon Kaufman will recognize his influence on my thinking about the incomprehensible mystery of God. Ronald Thiemann may recall specific conversations that brought me back to reconsider the details of Christian scripture and its life-shaping potential. Others have taught by example what it means to be theologically honest in a religiously plural world. I thank them all for their private conversations and public writings that inform what follows in this book.

I am grateful to Harvard Divinity School for providing institutional support and the collegial testing ground for my ideas. I am aware of various forums that have refined my thinking (including the annual meeting of the Catholic Theological Association of America and Our Lady of Czestochowa Parish); and the many institutions that have opened their doors to provide quiet spaces for reflection and writing (especially the College of New Rochelle, New York, and St. Peter's College in Jersey City, New Jersey).

I would like to acknowledge also my colleagues at Fordham University in New York City. Their intellectual engagement has helped to fuel this project in its last stages. My students also have helped to shape the presentation of this text and helped me to understand its purpose, especially members of Faith and Critical Reason and those students who accompanied me to the 2004 Parliament of the World's Religions.

Many members of my family have helped me make the connections between the academic world and the audience of others who might be interested in this work. Their frequent questions and sustained conversations have been an important source of encouragement. My thanks to them for this, and for the years of nurturing which have brought me to this place.

On the professional level, I am indebted to my editor, Justus George Lawler, whose insights, expertise and patience guided this manuscript through many drafts.

On the most personal level, I owe so much of this accomplishment to my husband, Michael Fletcher. He has been untiring in his support of this book. He has also helped me to find the quiet space of rivers where new thoughts could flow. His companionship, sacrifices, support and centering presence provided the context in which my work could develop. My deepest thanks to Michael and Owen for giving me the time to devote to my work and for creating a home full of laughter to which I could return.

Chapter One

THEOLOGICAL RESOURCES

T HERE IS A MYSTERY that Christians call "God." It is the mystery that is the origin of being; and ultimately, the mystery that governs the end of existence. In between the origin and the end, humans encounter this mystery in the workings of the world. It is glimpsed in the intricate design of a spider's web and in the division of cells that creates new life. It overwhelms the mind in the calculations of the galaxies and astounds the senses in the hurricane's force. It whispers its presence in the gentle trickle of a mountain stream. Mystery accompanies the search for meaning as persons ask: Where did we come from? Ultimately where are we going? Does it make any difference what sort of life we lead in the time in between? As the answers are tentative, symbolic and filled with uncertainty, mystery is encountered in the innermost depths of the self as persons seek to live authentic lives. Hints of the mystery show themselves daily in the countenance of human beings. Face to face with mystery at every turn, humans try to explain what they can and produce the explorations of science, philosophy, history, the arts and the many different forms of knowledge that try to situate the human condition in the world. Yet, as humans give voice to the reality of their existence, it is always against the backdrop of ultimate mystery. Human knowledge can trace the patterns of nature, but explanations cannot help but be incomplete. Science knows that the joining of a sperm and egg creates a new human being, but how this was designed and from where the personhood of the new individual emerges is beyond the reach of scientific explanation. When nature's force is evident in the hurricanes that blow across the ocean or the dry seasons that

eliminate whole crops, meteorologists can follow and even anticipate these patterns, but their incomplete explanation as to why this
particular pattern occurs in this particular time and place affect-
ing precisely those persons whose paths it crosses, again points to
the limits of human understanding. Philosophy offers insights into
human nature but cannot definitively say how human nature came
into being, that is, how we got here. History traces the patterns of
where we have been, but cannot ultimately say where we are going. These projects provide orienting points of reference, yet there
remains a fundamental question at the imaginative edge of all seeking: Does this existence look out onto ultimate nothingness, or is
there a reality that sustains all that is? Put another way, does human
existence boil down to ultimate meaninglessness, or is this existence
saturated with purpose and meaning?

The fundamental position of faith for Christians is to answer that
the universe ultimately has meaning; the unanswered questions have
answers, and the inexplicable origin and end holds its own explanation. For Christians, existence does not look out onto ultimate
nothingness, but expands out into the ultimate mystery to which
Christians have given the name "God." "God" is the mystery in
which we live and move and have our being. Fumbling for explanations, intuiting a reality greater than ourselves, humans attempt
the ultimate explanations of existence in talk about God.

Christians throughout the centuries have been reasonably confident in affirming that the word "God" points to something that is
real. They have been certain enough to say, "God exists." Contemporary Christians can also be reasonably confident in this assertion
when they follow the tradition of arguing for God's existence from
the reality of things in the world. Unless one is willing to take an
absolutist, nonfoundational stance, the foundation of theological
thinking can simply be that "reality exists." That is, there is something real about the material world and human beings within it.
If creation exists, it has arisen from some source. It is this creative source that the term "God" represents. The assertion that
"God exists" is most basically the assertion that creation arises
from somewhere, however mysterious and inaccessible that source
remains. God is the context of existence, source that creates things

as they are, and sustaining force that maintains all being. Or as Pseudo-Dionysius tries to explain,

> He is the Source and the measure of all the ages. He is the reality beneath time and the eternity behind being. He is the time within which things happen. He is being for whatever is. He is coming-to-be amid whatever happens. From him who is come eternity, essence and being, come time, genesis and becoming. He is the being immanent in and underlying things which are, however they are.[1]

With Pseudo-Dionysius, Christians have used the term "God" to represent the origin and creative force of being for all that exists. In the most basic way of speaking, this is the identification of God as creator. God exists as creator because creation exists. Of this, Christians have been reasonably confident.

I say that Christians throughout the centuries have been "reasonably confident" about God as the creative source of existence because knowledge of the source is always indirect and incomplete. As Thomas Aquinas explains, "Now because we do not know the essence of God the proposition ["God exists"] is not self-evident to us, but needs to be demonstrated by things that are more known to us, though less known in their nature — namely, by His effects."[2] When speaking of the mystery of existence, Christians use words about God fumblingly to speak of their experience of the power in creation and its ultimate origin. Yet, the power in creation remains elusive and the ultimate origin beyond human reach.

The reasonable assertion that "God exists" develops further into the Christian faith-stance that God as creator has brought creation into being with purpose and order to it. If the fundamental question of faith is whether this existence looks out onto ultimate nothingness or an ultimate reality that can be named "God," the answer that the Christian faith tradition has given is that at the edge of existence there is a creative source which has called all things into being in a purposeful way. This is a faith-stance that is one of hope rather than certainty, since the experience of the world often points in a different direction. In fact, the human experience of disorientation, unknowing and not being in control of existence can lead just as easily to the conclusion that the universe exists in a state of randomness. The position of Christian faith is to trust against the grain of these experiences and to see a coherent picture in the complex realities of our world. As Karl Rahner writes,

> ...the reality of the universe is in fact totally different from what [the] experience of our nothingness and forlornness in a cosmos ruthlessly going its way tries to make us believe. First, because this enormous power and energy that posits the cosmos in its reality and keeps unfolding it into an endlessly growing diversity is the most simple, most radical unity. This unity does not itself expand with the cosmos and thus disintegrate with it into multiplicity, but as one and as a whole, it is everywhere totally present at every point of the cosmos. This primordial power, which as an undivided totality subsists omnipotently everywhere at every point, we call *God*.[3]

Illuminating Christian doctrine, Rahner understands God as the source of a cosmos that is coherent because it is the very expression of God. God communicates Godself in and through creation, coming into self-expression in the multiplicity of a complex world. God, as the primordial power, unfolds Godself in and through the realities of the world. This force of creation does not dissipate into unconnected entities; rather, the primordial power, called God, "subsists omnipotently everywhere at every point." All of creation is understood as a communication of Godself, joining God and world in close proximity and recognizing the presence of God as grace abounding in creation. Coming into existence as the self-communication of God, all creation is situated as part of the graced reality of God and possesses something of the divine mystery within it.

The close link of creation and creator in the Christian frame of thinking provides a point of access to the mysterious reality of God. Christians throughout the centuries have continued to affirm what Paul writes in a letter to one of the earliest Christian communities: "Ever since the creation of the world [God's] eternal power and divine nature, invisible though they are, have been understood and seen through the things he has made" (Rom. 1:20). So while God

remains hidden from humanity, Christians have understood that
God reveals Godself in and through the created world and thus
name God through the things evident in creation. The tradition of
naming God through the things of creation abounds in the text of
the Bible, where the writers of the Hebrew Scriptures and Christian
New Testament try to point to the mystery of God in language
drawn from experience in the world. Once again, Pseudo-Dionysius
is helpful here, having culled the lines of scripture to create a list of
ways to speak of God:

> ...they give it many names, such as "I am being," "life,"
> "light," "God," the "truth." These same wise writers, when
> praising the Cause of everything that is, use names drawn from
> all the things caused: good, beautiful, wise, beloved, God of
> gods, Lord of Lords, Holy of Holies, eternal, existent, Cause
> of the ages. They call him source of life, wisdom, mind, word,
> knower, possessor beforehand of all the treasures of knowl-
> edge, power, powerful, and King of Kings, ancient of days, the
> unaging and unchanging, salvation, righteousness and sancti-
> fication, redemption, greatest of all and yet the one in the
> still breeze. They say he is in our minds, in our souls, and in
> our bodies, in heaven and on earth, that while remaining ever
> within himself he is also in and around and above the world,
> that he is above heaven and above all being, that he is sun,
> star, and fire, water, wind, and dew, cloud, archetypal stone,
> and rock, that he is all, that he is no thing.[4]

This list from scripture — and Pseudo-Dionysius offers a textual
reference for each one — enumerates the way in which the term
"God" functions in Christian thought. God is the source of all
that this — eternal, existent, Cause of the ages, ancient of days,
unaging, unchanging, source of life. The list includes powerful and
multiple images that reflect the idea that the mysterious reality of
God is evident in creation. God is life, light, sun, star, fire, water,
wind, dew and cloud. The term "God" refers to the source of existence and the mysterious reality that courses through creation.
But God also relates to the characteristics of order, purpose and
meaning in the world as represented in the qualities that endure —

the good, the beautiful, wisdom, righteousness and truth. Christian scripture presents the image of God as the source of an ordered and meaningful creation.

In affirming a meaningful existence sustained by God, Christians in the tradition have recognized that the ultimate meaning may be elusive for humans. Evidence of God as purposeful creator does not necessarily entail access to an understanding of the ultimate purpose. Put another way, affirming a design to God's creation does not guarantee understanding that design. This means that while humanity participates in the mystery of God as part of graced creation, humanity remains unable to fully comprehend the mystery of which it is a part. God remains beyond the powers of human control and understanding. The insufficiencies of scientific explanation, the wonder and awe humans feel at the hands of nature, and the limit-experiences that defy rationalization are component parts of the human experience that can be rendered in theological thinking as the affirmation that God is beyond human control and outside the grasp of human explanations. And it is not only modern science and reflection that has recognized the limits of the human reach. The depths of this experience extend back into the tradition of the Hebrew Scriptures where humans gave voice to the experience of not being in control and not fully understanding the mysterious powers of creation. For example, when Job sends up a lament from a life that has been wrecked by the powers of nature — he has been afflicted with "loathsome sores" (2:7), fire from heaven has destroyed his crops (1:16) and wind from the desert has killed his children (1:19) — it is God who replies. And God simply says: "Where were you when I laid the foundation of the earth?" (Job 38:4) This powerful and direct question identifies God as the source of creation and a force far greater than humanity. The design and origin of existence precedes human participation in it and remains beyond human control. God is like no other reality that humans encounter. In the writings of Isaiah this sentiment is voiced as God says, "To whom then will you compare me, or who is my equal? says the Holy One.... The Lord is the everlasting God, the Creator of the ends of the earth. He does not faint or grow weary; his understanding is unsearchable" (Isa. 40:25, 28). Through poetics and personification, the writers of the Hebrew Scriptures express what humans throughout the centuries have come to realize: we are part of an existence that we do not fully understand. Paul's letter to the community at Rome affirms this idea when it includes passages from this same chapter of Isaiah.

> O the depths of the riches and wisdom and knowledge of God! How unsearchable are his judgments and how inscrutable his ways! "For who has known the mind of the Lord? Or who has been his counselor?" (Rom. 11:33–34)

Like the first Christians to whom Paul addresses these words, Christians today live in a world that remains a mystery. God is the source and force of that mystery. Thus, while God reveals Godself in and through a meaningful creation, and humans can speak of this mysterious reality of God, in the end, God cannot be fully understood, or in fact, captured by human speech. As Gregory of Nyssa explains, the reality of God is "incapable of being grasped by any term, or any idea, or any other conception."[5] In fact, no human speech can adequately express this mystery. In Pseudo-Dionysius's words again,

> ... the inscrutable One is out of the reach of every rational process. Nor can any words come up to the inexpressible Good, this One, this Source of all unity, this supra-existent Being. Mind beyond mind, word beyond speech, it is gathered up by no discourse, by no intuition, by no name. It is and it is as no other being is. Cause of all existence, and therefore itself transcending existence, it alone could give an authoritative account of what it really is.[6]

And so, there is a tension. On the one hand, Christians understand God through creation; on the other, humans can never comprehend God. In one breath Christians attempt to speak of the mystery, and in the next recognize the limits of speech in this capacity. The dual trajectories — God as known and unknown, God as hidden and revealed, God as spoken and unspeakable — live vibrantly in the patterns of Christian thought. The tension inherent in Christian talk about God gives evidence of the way God is mystery in the tradition. God reveals Godself in and through creation, yet remains hidden to humans as creatures. This hiddenness is God's mystery. Humans speak of God in words that try to communicate how God has revealed Godself, yet human words can neither capture nor fully communicate the reality of God. This inability to communicate God's reality reflects the mystery. The projects of human knowledge present creation as a context which can be understood by human persons within it; explained theologically, this reflects how humanity is part of a graced creation that is self-gift of God. Yet, there are limits to what humans can understand and control of this graced creation. The limits of human understanding of the creation of which they are a part means that all human existence is conditioned by mystery. The give and take, hiddenness and revelation, known and unknown of God represent the essential tension that is mystery within the Christian tradition.

There are both positive and negative ways of employing "mystery" as a theological theme. If the tension of knowing and unknowing is left as a contradiction, the facile answer, "It is mystery," can be used to limit theological thinking. Such an answer suggests to the seeker to give up any search because what is not understood simply cannot be understood. In a maneuver that silences the searcher, "mystery" stands as a giant question mark that is left simply at that. God as mystery can make God absent in the process. God beyond human grasp can distance humans from the reality of God and frustrate authentic seeking. There is, however, a more positive way to use the concept of mystery which is quite the opposite. Rather than a creativity-stifling contradiction, Christian God-talk can be read as a creative tension. This follows strands of the tradition where mystery is not the giant question mark that ends all questions; instead mystery is more like a complex puzzle that the mind wrestles to wrap itself around, intriguing precisely because it is beyond the easy grasp and engaging as it encourages the mind to know it more deeply.

This way of understanding "mystery" can be seen in the work of Pseudo-Dionysius quoted above. As Janet Williams explains,

> The whole thrust of Dionysius' account of religious language
> is that divine reality eludes its grasp. God transcends all being,

all created things, and no words and concepts derived from them could ever fit God. Indeed, the very process of spiritual growth is a process of negotiation of such words and concepts, each providing a limited theophany which is to be appreciated and then gone beyond.[7]

Spiritual growth consists in recognizing the names given to God as manifestations of the mystery, yet always going beyond them to ever new revelations of God. Human words drawn from created realities are useful for opening humans up to God, but importantly, they are transcended toward further recognition of what is infinitely unknown. As two movements, affirmation in the names of God and the counter-affirmation that God cannot finally be named work together to bring humans to a greater awareness that there is always more that is not known of God. In order for each name to be an authentic theophany and not merely empty human speech, each must reveal something about God. Yet, in order for God to be God in essential mystery, the names cannot contain all of who God is. God is incomprehensible mystery.

This way of understanding God as incomprehensible mystery is best presented by Thomas Aquinas in his *Summa Theologica*. Here, Aquinas explains God's incomprehensibility by beginning counter-intuitively with the idea that God can be known. In fact, for Aquinas, God is "supremely knowable." And yet, because of the infinite abundance of what there is to know of God, humans are incapable of supremely knowing God. As Aquinas explains,

> Every thing is knowable according to its actuality. But God, Whose being is infinite . . . is infinitely knowable. Now no created intellect can know God infinitely. . . . Hence it is impossible that [any created intellect] should comprehend God.[8]

Thinking of the mystery of God in this way, the term "God" indicates a reality whose essence breaks the bounds of what the human mind can contain. As Aquinas puts it, " . . . what is supremely knowable in itself may not be knowable to a particular intellect, because of the excess of the intelligible object above the intellect; as for example, the sun, which is supremely visible, cannot be seen by the bat by reason of its excess of light."[9] Just as the bat's sense of sight is overwhelmed in the excessive light of the sun, humanity's senses are overwhelmed by the reality of God. What there is to know of the ultimate source of existence and force that courses through creation is so expansive, so overwhelming and truly awesome that the mind cannot contain it. Continuing Aquinas's understanding of God's mystery, Karl Rahner explains that incomprehensibility "follows from the essential infinity of God which makes it impossible for a finite created intellect to exhaust the possibility of knowledge and truth contained in this absolute fullness of being."[10] God, as source of all existence and creative force that courses through creation, is unlimited being itself. It is overwhelming in its reality. This is why God remains beyond the limits of human understanding. Incomprehensibility is not so much a sad reflection on human limitedness, but rather the exuberant celebration of God's limitlessness, a limitlessness that calls the human person into ever new realizations of the awesome mystery of existence. Incomprehensibility means that the human person glimpses the mystery of God not as absence, but as overabundance.

When God's mystery is seen as overabundance, humanity is offered innumerable opportunities to witness the limited theophanies of God. That which is glimpsed in nature, reflected in humanity and encountered at the imaginative edge of existence is a reality far greater than what the human mind can comprehend. But unlike the facile answer "it is a mystery" when it stifles the search, understanding God's mystery as overabundance invites the human response of always coming to know God more. Such a response to the unknown can be paralleled with the projects of human knowledge that span as far back as the origins of humanity and extend as far into the future as the imagination can see. As demonstrated in the patterns of science and other quests for understanding, humans certainly can explain some of their existence; and yet, the constant pursuit of new scientific investigations demonstrates that knowing *part* of reality does not constitute a mastery of *all* of reality. In creative tension with the unknown, humans continually strive to know more about their existence, recognizing the inability to finally know all that is to be known. While unable to finally comprehend or control the existence of which they are a part, humans nonetheless offer the answers of science, history, philosophy, psychology and the like as orientations to this mystery. So, too, with human strivings to understand the ultimate source of our existence, the reality that Christians name "God," the human response to the mystery of God is not to leave the mystery unexamined, but to strive always to know more, to experience the mystery ever more fully, and to orient ourselves through what can be known.

Up to this point, I have been employing the term "God" as it has been used by Christians throughout the centuries. I have underscored that the assertion that God is the creator of a purposeful existence is a distinctively Christian faith-stance in a universe that can be interpreted in a variety of ways. But now I'd like to follow Rahner as he uses the term "God" with a different emphasis. He argues that if "God" indeed points to the reality that brought all things into existence and continues to sustain them, then the reality pointed to with the term "God" can be (and is) experienced not only by Christians but by all human beings. In order to broaden the discussion of thinking about the mystery of God from a decidedly Christian perspective to one that could engage people of diverse faiths, I'd like to follow Rahner as he parallels the human striving for knowledge with human transcendence toward God. In this, Rahner argues for the universal experience of God.

When a skeptical conversation partner once said to Rahner, "I have never had an experience of God," Rahner simply replied, "I don't believe you; I just don't accept that. You have had, perhaps, no experience of God under this precise code-word *God*, but you have had or have now an experience of God — and I am convinced that this is true of every person."[11] In order to support such an assertion, Rahner saw the most basic human experiences as indicating an experience of God. The ability to know, to love and to make free choices represent, for Rahner, an opportunity for coming to an awareness of the incomprehensible mystery of God. Rahner begins with the experiences themselves and reasons *a posteriori* to the foundational mystery of God evident at the limits of human experience.

Every day, the human person has the opportunity for growth by engaging their ability to know, to love, and to make free choices. When a person goes outside himself in loving another, or expands her knowledge in the process of scientific exploration, or pursues a life choice not bound by the logic of a materialistic world, that individual extends beyond the limits of what he or she presently is and creates something new. When the limits of the self are transcended and something new is created, the individual has the opportunity to ask how this growth and transcendence is possible. There must be a reality outside the self which sustains this growth and knowledge. Deeper reflection encourages the individual to recognize that each discrete act of growth suggests that the source of growth is limitless, because the opportunities for love and the possibilities for learning can never be exhausted. The realization that human growth in transcendence is limitless brings humanity to an awareness of the limitless source of existence itself. This infinite source, which Rahner names "God," is experienced as the "something more" of human existence. In the process of transcendence humans do not arrive at an immediate experience or face-to-face encounter with God, rather, because the processes of transcendence are unlimited and essentially infinite, humans can reason after these experiences and arrive at an awareness of what necessarily must be the case: that there exists an infinite source of knowledge, will and love. When humans realize that growth is limitless, there comes an awareness also that the ultimate term toward which this growth is directed can never be grasped or understood. This ever-receding horizon of transcendence is what Rahner names God. He writes that we know God from our experience *a posteriori*, "only as the term of transcendence."[12] Thus, while God is present as grace in the very fundamental experiences that make us human, the fullness of the reality of God is always beyond human grasp.

Here, the essential tension surfaces again. Humans grow toward God in transcendence, but God forever remains as a horizon beyond human reach. Yet, ever more clearly now, the tension is creative. For just as humans strive toward God in their transcendence, the horizon of God's mystery becomes an ever-greater reality. As growth brings humanity closer to the abundant source of existence, it is revealed that this source can never be exhausted. The overabundance of God's mystery which remains forever beyond the horizon of human transcendence encourages humanity to seek, to love, to understand and to grow always more. It is precisely the never-ending quest for fulfillment — in knowledge, will and love — that makes humans fundamentally human. Thus, the creative tension of never grasping and never exhausting the reality of God, yet always striving and seeking represents the very process of growth that makes humans human. Human striving toward ever-greater becoming is human participation in the inexhaustible being of God. Human striving toward knowledge is human participation in the incomprehensible mystery that is God. The fullness of the creative tension comes in the intimate joining of God's reality and human being. Humans are most fully human and find their greatest satisfaction as they continually grow in knowledge, will and love. As the source of knowledge, will and love, God sustains this human growth and fulfillment. It is only by being overabundant, incomprehensible mystery that God can never-endingly sustain the human process of fulfillment. The creativity of the essential tension surfaces to insist that this inability to fully know God or to ever arrive at the horizon of God's being is not the source of eternal frustration. Rather, the experience of eternal contemplation and growth is fulfilling in itself. As Aquinas describes of the intellectual process,

> Nothing can be wearisome that is wonderful to him that looks on it, because as long as we wonder at it, it still moves our desire. Now the created intellect always looks with wonder on the divine substance, since no created intellect can comprehend it. Therefore, the intellectual substance cannot possibly become weary of that vision.[13]

In Aquinas's description of the beatific vision, the human faculties remain active and find happiness in the unceasing activity of contemplating God. God's overabundant nature remains incomprehensible as it forever moves the intellect's desire to know it and satisfies the mind in the experience of wonder. Even in the eschaton — in "salvation" or "heaven" — humanity enjoys an ever-deepening knowledge of God, which is never exhausted. God's infinity expands the possibilities for coming to know God and for knowing God for eternity. This overabundant incomprehensibility is characteristic of God so that even beyond the confines of human existence in time and space, humans will experience God as overwhelming abundance and incomprehensible mystery. According to Rahner,

> The incomprehensibility of God should not then be regarded as a distant reality, for it increases rather than diminishes in the vision of God, in which alone it becomes an inescapable event. It does not describe the remnants of something which, sadly, remains unknown, but rather points to the immediate object of the experience of God in heaven, an object which is present in the mind overflowing with the fullness of God's self-communication.[14]

Christians, in the tradition of Aquinas and Rahner, have understood the mystery of God arising from the overabundance of the reality pointed to with the term. Like the bat overwhelmed by light, the mind overflowing in contemplating God or, in the metaphor of Teresa of Avila, just as a sponge becomes saturated with water, the soul overflows with divinity when face to face with the mystery of God.[15] God's incomprehensible mystery is encountered as overabundance that fills humanity to its depths and then overflows. There is no end to the being, fullness and mystery of God.

It is from the starting point of God's mystery as incomprehensible overabundance that I begin to reflect on a Christian response to religious diversity. Just as knowledge of all things is constructed against the backdrop of ultimate mystery, so too the consideration of the reality of different religions is conditioned by this same unknowing. If the term "God" is the Christian way of referring to the creative source and unending force within creation that is universally accessible, then people of other faiths might have a different term to refer to this same reality. If Christians have affirmed something about the mystery of God through their particular tradition, and if God's mystery is the result of God's overabundance, then perhaps other religious traditions have insights to be affirmed of this mysterious overabundance as well. In engaging with people of other faiths, Christians might be opened up to the never-ending possibilities that arise from the overabundant, incomprehensible mystery of God. Each of the diverse representations of this mystery — in human knowledge, Christian God-talk and insights from the many religions of the world — might be understood in the tradition of Pseudo-Dionysius's "limited theophanies." Each might be considered a way of communicating something real about the mystery of existence which nonetheless does not capture all of the reality, the ultimate reality, of this existence. The creative tension of ever-new revelations of the incomprehensible mystery of God opens up infinitely to new ways of understanding, approaching and considering the mystery of our existence.

Broadening the creative tension to include insights from the diverse religions of the world raises a particular set of challenges for Christian theological thinking. These challenges can be distilled into three fundamental issues. First, there must be ways of listening to people of other faiths. This can be a real challenge since diverse traditions have said different things about the mystery that Christians call "God." Embedded in different cultural patterns and linguistic systems, diverse experiences of the mystery of existence often appear to be incommensurable and impossible to negotiate. Nevertheless, in order to be enriched by diverse religions, there need to be strategies for hearing the insights of people of other faiths and learning from their unique perspectives. The second challenge is that while listening to new perspectives from other faiths, Christians cannot lose sight of the distinctively Christian way of experiencing the mystery in the life and person of Jesus of Nazareth. Going back to the earliest Christian texts in scripture, Christians find clear affirmations that God is uniquely known in and through Jesus. These affirmations include: "...no one knows the Father except the Son and anyone to whom the Son chooses to reveal him" (Matt. 11:27), and "No one has ever seen God. It is God the only Son, who is close to the Father's heart, who has made him known" (John 1:18; echoed in John 5:37–38; 6:46; 8:19). Christ is seen as "the image of God" (2 Cor. 4:4) or more precisely, "the image of the invisible God" (Col. 1:15). For Christians, the incomprehensible God is revealed to humanity in and through the person of Jesus of Nazareth. Thus,

the first two criteria in constructing a theology of religious pluralism are (1) that it offer strategies for engaging with people of other
faiths in their distinctiveness and (2) that it maintain the Christian
affirmations of what is known of God through Jesus.

Unfortunately, the affirmations about Jesus have historically been
a stumbling block in Christian relations with people of other faiths.
Claims of uniqueness and ultimacy for Jesus Christ have often
drowned out other voices. This is because the affirmation that the
incomprehensible God is known in and through Jesus of Nazareth
comes with an additional affirmation: that God's ultimate design in
creating humanity is to bring all people to salvation, and, importantly, Jesus is the mediator of that salvation. With this affirmation,
Christians have asserted a certain knowability of the design of the
mysterious creator. This is the heart of the Christian affirmation
that challenges Christians in understanding other faiths. It is seen,
for example, in the letter to Timothy, which asserts:

> [God our Savior] desires everyone to be saved and to come to
> the knowledge of the truth. For there is one God; there is also
> one mediator between God and humankind, Christ Jesus....
> (1 Tim. 2:4–5)

Another way of framing this has been to say that the way to the
incomprehensible God is in and through Jesus himself. The words
placed on the lips of Jesus in John's gospel point to this affirmation
with powerful clarity, as Jesus proclaims,

> I am the way, and the truth, and the life. No one comes to the
> Father except through me. If you know me, you will know my
> Father also. From now on you do know him and have seen
> him. (John 14:6–7)

Christians down through the centuries have held this affirmation
firmly in their thinking about God. For Christians, the invisible God
of scripture, the incomprehensible God of tradition is known in
and through Jesus of Nazareth. In contemplating the universe and
the place of humans within it, Christians have seen their purpose
identified with "salvation" (as fullness of union with God), and
"salvation" as accessible uniquely through Jesus Christ.

Because I am seeking new ways to listen to other faiths, it is necessary to scratch beneath the surface and ask what early Christians might have meant by this additional affirmation of God's salvation in Jesus Christ. It is clear from scripture that the earliest Christian communities saw "salvation" and the name "Jesus Christ" as intimately linked. But salvation in the name of Jesus Christ was not the utterance of that name only; it was linked to practices patterned on Jesus and continued after his death. For when, in Acts of the Apostles, Jesus' followers proclaim, "There is salvation in no one else, for there is no other name under heaven given among mortals by which we must be saved" (Acts 4:12), they are using this faith affirmation as a defense for healings they performed. With its link to the practice of healing, salvation is, for the author of Luke-Acts a "restoration to wholeness" with "the universality of salvation available in Christ for all human beings who turn to him."[16] This link between Jesus' saving activity and the actions of his followers is not only part of the imagined community that Acts represents, but is also found in letters to actual communities written by Paul. For example, in a letter to Christians at Philippi written sometime between the years 55 and 65 CE, Paul fosters a sense of solidarity and care among the members of the community with the words,

> Let each of you look not to your own interests, but to the interests of others. Let the same mind be in you that was in Christ Jesus, who, though he was in the form of God, did not regard equality with God as something to be exploited, but emptied himself, taking the form of a slave, being born in human likeness. And being found in human form, he humbled himself and became obedient to the point of death — even death on a cross.

> Therefore God also highly exalted him and gave him the name that is above every name, so that at the name of Jesus every knee should bend, in heaven and on earth and under the earth, and every tongue should confess that Jesus Christ is Lord, to the glory of God the Father.

Therefore, my beloved, just as you have always obeyed me, not only in my presence, but much more now in my absence, work out your own salvation with fear and trembling; for it is God who is at work in you, enabling you both to will and to work for his good pleasure.

Do all things without murmuring and arguing, so that you may be blameless and innocent, children of God without blemish in the midst of a crooked and perverse generation, in which you shine like stars in the world. (Phil. 2:4–13)

Christ's own practice, Paul recalls, was self-sacrificing even unto death, in such perfect obedience that God exalted Jesus, giving him "the name that is above every name, so that at the name of Jesus, every knee should bend, in heaven and on earth and under the earth, and every tongue should confess that Jesus Christ is Lord" (vv. 9–11). In the practice of humble service, Paul admonishes the community to "work out your own salvation" (v. 12). Thus we see that in this early letter the proclamation of Jesus' name above all other names is linked not only to salvation, but this salvation is linked to practices of humility and self-sacrifice. Paul uses the proclamation of Jesus' salvific activity to encourage this early community to "shine like stars in the world" (v. 15). The action of salvation — in humble service and healing practice — is carried on by Jesus' followers after his death. The call to "salvation" is an exhortation to wholeness and humility. Thus, for the earliest Christians, the way to the incomprehensible God is in and through Jesus of Nazareth and entails a commitment also to a way of living and practice. For Christians, salvation completes the circuit of affirmations because it suggests that orientation to the incomprehensible mystery and alignment with its reality comes from patterning one's life on the life and person of Jesus of Nazareth. If God is the source of all existence and yet ultimately incomprehensible to humanity, the knowledge of God accessible in the following of Jesus Christ aligns persons with the incomprehensible mystery of our existence. By following the pattern of Jesus of Nazareth, Christians orient themselves purposefully to the mystery of existence.

But the tradition of affirmations must be held in balance with the tradition of incomprehensibility. That is, knowledge of God through scripture and the person of Jesus Christ does not erase the incomprehensibility as overabundance that the tradition has also affirmed. Even in the New Testament affirmations about God's incomprehensibility exist alongside Christian affirmations of God's revelation in Jesus Christ. Paul affirms that God's wisdom is "secret and hidden" (1 Cor. 2:7), and the author of a letter to Timothy describes God as "invisible" (1 Tim. 1:17). The lines of Christian scripture echo the tradition that "No one has ever seen God" (John 1:18; 1 John 4:12). The gospel writers present incomprehensibility as an element of Jesus' own teaching when he explains that God's wisdom is out of the reach of even (or perhaps especially) "the wise and the intelligent" (Luke 10:21; Matt. 11:25). So, the creative tension continues even while affirming God's revealing Godself in the person of Jesus. As Karl Barth suggests, knowledge of God always remains an "enigma."[17] Barth writes, "It is not God who stands before us if He does not stand before us in such a way that He is and remains a mystery to us."[18]

This initial investigation of Christian God-talk suggests that the term "God" refers to the mystery of our existence that is its origin and end, its creator and source. And while affirming that this reality exists, the Christian tradition has also held God's ultimate incomprehensibility. But this incomprehensibility is not understood as a lack or void, rather as originating in God's overabundance. Like a bat overwhelmed by the light or a sponge overflowing with God's reality, the human mind cannot exhaust the reality of God in order to comprehend this infinite mystery. This overabundant mystery of our existence sustains our growth as the unlimited source of knowledge, will and love. This mystery is encountered in the basic human experiences and, for Christians, in the person of Jesus of Nazareth. Knowing God in Jesus presents a pattern of relating to the mystery of our existence — a pattern of self-giving love. But this pattern and knowledge of God in Jesus Christ does not erase God's incomprehensibility. Incomprehensibility is maintained to the end of existence and beyond as coming to know the mystery is humanity's essential drive and ultimate fulfillment.

This exploration has provided some initial suggestions that there might be resources within the Christian tradition that can help twenty-first-century Christians formulate a response to persons of other faiths. Affirmation about God's revelation in Jesus' pattern of self-giving love sets Christians on an orienting path to the mystery of existence. At the same time, God's overabundant incomprehensibility means that God's reality is never exhausted in human knowledge of God, rather, there is forever the opportunity for coming to know God more fully. This suggests that Christians might open to the possibility of diverse reflections on the incomprehensible mystery of God that arise from other traditions. Incomprehensibility as over-abundance suggests that there might be distinctive encounters with the mystery that Christians call "God" as it is experienced by people of other faiths. If human fulfillment is found in the process of coming to know God, then ever-new affirmations about God could be embraced as new pathways on the theological journey. It would seem that this embracing of incomprehensibility and affirmation could open powerful opportunities for Christians to encounter persons of other faiths. For it is precisely the case that other faith traditions offer different affirmations about the infinite, mysterious reality which Christians name "God." It would seem that Christians today and throughout history could welcome new and diverse insights from our neighbors of other faiths so as to deepen and continue the eternal process of coming to know God.

While this may be a fruitful stance for Christians of the twenty-first century (and I will return to it in the closing chapters), such openness to persons of other faiths and welcoming of the resources for exploring new ways of understanding God has been the norm neither in Christianity's ancient nor recent past. The flow of history in affirming God's revelation in Jesus Christ and salvation as part of that revelation has tended to emphasize affirmation over incomprehensibility, precisely when Christians consider "salvation" and the fate of persons of other faiths.

When earlier I suggested that there were three fundamental issues in hearing the insights of religious others on the mystery of God, I indicated only two: the need for (1) strategies for hearing the "other" and (2) ways of maintaining what has been affirmed about God through the person of Jesus. The third fundamental issue that completes the picture is that these strategies must also recognize that hearing the insights of the religious other always takes place in a complex nexus of personal, social, political *and* religious contexts where listening to the other does not have only religious consequences but social, political and personal ones as well. Thus, while this chapter has established the dual trajectories of incomprehensibility and affirmation as both central to the Christian tradition, the next step in this exploration is to see whether and how this balance has been maintained in lived contexts. Chapter 2 will consider the resource of Christian history as providing patterns and pitfalls for understanding religious difference. In it, I will investigate when and how Christians have met people of other faiths in history. In the meetings, I will look for strategies that enabled Christians to hear their neighbors, and those actions and attitudes that stifled the other's voice. From these patterns in history, Christians today might find resources for their own response to religious difference.

Chapter Two

HISTORICAL RESOURCES

W HEN CHRISTIANS TODAY attempt to formulate a response to
religious diversity, they look to the past for precedents. The
exploration of chapter 1 has demonstrated that the themes of God's
incomprehensibility and positive affirmations about God can inform
contemporary theological thinking. By looking to the past, patterns
of action are also evident that might provide resources for constructing a response to religious difference. And so, this chapter looks to
history for the "Christian" response to neighbors of other faiths, as
these responses have been lived out in actual contexts.

I put the word "Christian" in quotation marks to draw attention
to a few important realities about this reconstruction of Christian
history. First, is to recognize the impossible task of identifying *the*
Christian response in history as if there were one response formulated and applied in every encounter of the last two thousand years.
There is, of course, not one Christian response, but in fact innumerable and diverse responses formulated by different persons in
different social and historical contexts. And so, to accurately present
the "Christian" response to religious difference would require a
God's-eye view in order to communicate the rich diversity and multiplicity of ways actual Christians in context have responded to their
neighbors of other faiths. This we don't have. Any reconstruction
of history will necessarily select some actors to the exclusion of
others, and so the reader will recognize from the outset that the
episodes presented in these pages do not exhaust the many and diverse responses that Christians have formulated. The discussion of
this chapter is further complicated by the fact that access to these
particular Christians has been, in part, predetermined by limitations

placed in the past. Historians have already made editorial decisions to write about some events and not others, to focus on some actors and not others, and so they have bequeathed access to the voice, experience and response of some Christians and not others. Ever new work in historical reconstruction can make available new resources to consider in the future. For the time being, recognizing these limitations, this chapter will nevertheless trace some responses of some Christians to give insight into the possibilities for contemporary encounters.

Mapping *some* of the responses in history is an important task for a number of reasons. First and foremost, the past functions as legitimating for the present. This is very much the case in theological thinking where past discussions on Christian themes serve as precedents for theological thinking across twenty-plus centuries. Just as chapter 1 traced theological writings of the past to establish a Christian pattern of thought, so too, evidence of past actions serves as a component of the Christian tradition that is a resource for today. By calling to mind the ways actual Christians in actual contexts have responded to the reality of religious difference, one might find some possibilities for today in the precedents of the past. Yet, memory does not only serve the empowering function of providing patterns of action for today. The past also serves as a "dangerous memory" warning of pitfalls to avoid. The dual possibilities — both positive and negative — reflect a second reason why "Christian" has been placed in quotation marks. That is, the responses crafted by some Christians have been, well, less than Christian. If "Christian" means patterned on the life and practice of Jesus Christ, it is no new revelation that some of the responses of actual Christians have fallen short of this criterion. Presenting the good and the bad of Christian history simply serves as a reminder that theological thinking has material consequences and that these consequences are ones that impact others.

In thinking about the power and problems of using history for contemporary reflection, Elisabeth Schüssler Fiorenza writes, "Historical interpretation is defined by contemporary questions and horizons of reality and conditioned by contemporary political interests and structures of domination."[1] In earlier times, the investigation into historical encounters was shaped by interests in discovering the Christian perspective on things. Christians were often seen as the sole actors in these accounts, while persons of other faiths were constructed as mute objects to be encountered. Today, there is increasing recognition that encounters are always shaped by both partners; the authentic response to persons of other faiths comes out of a dialogue. The desire to take into account the perspective of the other today suggests also that the history to be constructed might also take into account the perspective of the other. Yet, since so many of the sources of Christian history were written solely with an interest in the one-sided Christian perspective, the other side of the experience has been lost. To remedy this, postcolonial theorist Homi K. Bhabha suggests a strategy of reading against the grain of Christian texts to hear the voice of the other captured there.[2] By witnessing how Christians react to religious others, an imaginative reconstruction can present what the encounter may have been from the others' perspectives. By applying this strategy to the texts of Christian history both sides of the encounter can be reconstructed, at least in part.

By journeying into the past, then, I hope to uncover the possibilities and pitfalls in patterns of Christian response to religious difference. But, unlike earlier histories, I am interested not only in the Christian perspective on the encounter, but also the experience and insight of persons of other faiths. By considering new perspectives on these encounters, I hope to broaden the understanding of their complexity and diversity and to see resources for patterning anew a Christian response to religious difference.

To trace Christian responses to religious otherness, one can return all the way to the origins of Christianity itself. For as long as there have been Christians, their identity has been formed in contact and conversation with religious "others." These "others" were, in the first instance, not so other, as Christian identity developed as a conversation among Jews. Jesus of Nazareth, as a particular Jew responding to the particular Judaism of his time and place, sought to reinvigorate it with a new sense of God's nearness and concern for the well-being of humanity. Challenging ritual laws and reaching

out to the marginalized, Jesus can be seen as promoting the wholeness of human beings as a religious enterprise. But this enterprise
challenged also the social and political order of his day, ultimately
leading to his death under the political authority of the Roman Empire. Those who carried on his mission in the Jesus Movement after
his death did so as Jews, seeing the pattern of Jesus' life in faithful continuity with what was beloved in their Jewish heritage. As
early Christians integrated their "Jesus" identity into their "Jewish"
identity, contact between "Jewish-Christians" and "Jews" would
have taken place in ritual and social spaces. Throughout the ancient world, Jewish Christians continued to attend synagogues and
were members of the wider Jewish community for at least a few
generations. These Christians formulated their understanding of
religious distinctiveness in conversation and continuity with their
Jewish self-understanding. They were both Jewish and Christian simultaneously. How did the first Christians respond to the Jewish
faith? The varied relationships between Jews and Christians are reflected in the texts of the New Testament. Alan Segal uses these texts
and the resources of historical scholarship to reconstruct these relationships in his book, *Rebecca's Children: Judaism and Christianity
in the Roman World*. As Segal reconstructs, the earliest Christians
would have been active in the religious life of local synagogues. But
from the perspective of many rabbis, Christianity might have been
seen as a Jewish heresy and thus Christians might have been under-
standably barred from positions of influence by rabbis who limited
their roles in synagogue services.[3] The affirmation of Jesus as re-
vealer of God and as one with God compromised the monotheism
that stands at the heart of Jewish faith. But the first generation
of Christians did not see this conflict in the same way as some
of their Jewish synagogue leaders, and thus continued to identify
as both Jewish and Christian. As Segal describes the situation, the
polemical passages in the New Testament constitute a "family affair" that is, a conflict and debate within the Jewish community and
its Christian sect. These family conflicts come in different shades —
from Matthew's apparent dispute between Jewish-Christians and
the Pharisaic leadership, to John's gospel that reflects the stance
of a group which had broken entirely from Judaism. In framing

the relationship between Judaism and Christianity in antiquity as a "family affair," Segal suggests that the two traditions became twin children with different missions. The Christian mission of universal conversion stood in direct conflict with the Jewish mission of holiness among the chosen people. Once the communities "divorced," stronger boundaries of difference were erected between them from ancient times onward. The new affirmation of God's revelation in Jesus Christ was so utterly central to Christian identity that this affirmation about God divided Jewish-Christians from their Jewish family members and friends. From the perspective of Jews of the day, undoubtedly, this affirmation compromised the transcendence and even the incomprehensibility of God.

Among the earliest Christian texts are Paul's writings to the first Christian communities throughout the Mediterranean world. These are often imbued with a deep sense of his own Jewish heritage and communicate the importance of Jesus through the lens of the Jewish faith. But Paul was writing not only to early Christians in Jewish contexts, in fact, very often he was writing to Christians in other parts of the Mediterranean world whose religious identities would not have been shaped in synagogues but in contact with practitioners of Greek and Roman religion. How did these early Christians respond to their neighbors of other faiths? Their responses must have been embedded in their ongoing social lives, as new converts to Christianity continued to be members of the wider social organization of ancient cities. In Paul's letters, there is evidence that these Christians continued to share meals with their neighbors of other faiths, even in the houses of worship of the Greek religious tradition. In the ancient world, meat was available after it had been sacrificed in these temples, and the surplus was sold by local priests. The reality was that as Greeks adopted Christian identity and practice, this did not cancel out their social-location as members of families and associates in the wider community. They would still be asked to celebratory meals and family gatherings that would take place in the communal dining areas of temples. The question that arose among these early Christians was whether or not is was acceptable to eat this meat and share meals with their neighbors of another faith. Paul's letters to the communities at Corinth and Rome respond to this practice of eating food "sacrificed to idols" (1 Cor. 8; Rom. 14). Paul diplomatically leaves open the possibility of accepting these invitations and sharing meals in non-Christian houses of worship suggesting that Christians indeed gathered for meals in temples alongside their non-Christian friends. One must imagine that conversations across the table at times turned to religion and that these Christians articulated the vision of their newly formed faith in contact with others. These ancient Christians learned also from their conversations with non-Christians, incorporating Greek and Roman elements into the Christian tradition.

In other cities of the Mediterranean world, Christians had opportunities to come into contact with additional faith traditions. In North Africa, for example, at the crossroads of Roman trade routes, ancient Christians might have encountered the faiths of Asia as tradespeople and travelers arrived in the thriving metropolis of Alexandria. There is evidence of this as the theologian and spokesperson for the Christian faith, Clement of Alexandria (c. 160–215), identifies the Buddha as a holy figure for persons in India and distinguishes the brahmin leaders of Hindu practice as well.[4] Clearly, Christians in antiquity developed their faith affirmations aware of counter-affirmations in other communities of faith. It was these counter-affirmations that often forced Christian thinkers to articulate the distinctiveness of the Christian pattern of thought and practice, a distinctiveness not only vis-à-vis Jewish and Greek patterns, but also in response to the diverse traditions of the East.

In the ancient Mediterranean world, information and travel systems were already bringing religious difference into Christian awareness. But with the Roman trade routes extending beyond the empire, there exists the possibility that Christians in the earliest centuries encountered people of other faiths in *their* native lands. Such a possibility undergirds the tradition of the Acts of Thomas, which places the apostle Thomas in India in the year 52 CE. While the dating of Christian arrival with Thomas in the first century cannot be proven beyond the status of legend, the text of Acts of Thomas (dated to the second or third century) provides evidence that a group of early Christians envisioned contact with the people of India informed by their distinctive Christian story.[5] Paralleling the stories of Acts of the Apostles, the Acts of Thomas sees the apostle Thomas sent by the risen Christ to bring the gospel to India. Reluctantly, he goes. While there, he is employed as a carpenter and architect for a native king who commissions him to build an inspiring palace. Thomas agrees, accepts the money from the king and heads off to a further point in the kingdom to begin construction. As the episodes of the story pass, Thomas frequently asks the king for more money to continue building the palace; the king gives it to him. But what the king doesn't know is that Thomas is using the money to feed the poor. The text reads, "And [the king] was sending silver and gold from time to time. But Judas [Thomas] was going about the villages and cities and was ministering to the poor, and was making the afflicted comfortable. . . . "[6] When the king finds out, he is furious and brings Thomas in for questioning. This is Thomas's reply:

"I have built thee the palace."

The king saith to him: "In what time can we go (and) look at it?"

Judas saith to him: "Thou canst not see it now, but when thou hast departed from this world."[7]

The "palace" Judas Thomas builds on earth could be construed as the kingdom of God Jesus preached and enacted in his ministry. This passage reflects the idea that salvation includes the well-being of persons in this world, as the "palace" Thomas promises to the king is beyond this life but directly related to the good Thomas has undertaken with the money given him by the king. As an early text depicting the encounter of a Christian among persons of other faiths in India, it is important to note that at no point are those whom Thomas serves identified as Christian. The role of Thomas's mission is the well-being of the native people, in essence, people of other faiths. Thomas travels throughout India self-identifying as "a liberator of many"; others see him as a compassionate healer whose work is done without any recompense.[8] The text of these Acts of Thomas reflects the views of a Christian community in the second century who apparently saw the role of Christians as fostering the well-being of others, regardless of their faith perspective. What it meant to affirm Jesus as Messiah was to carry on his work of healing in the world.

From these locations in Christian antiquity, a conversation between Christians and people of other faiths echoes down through the centuries. This conversation is a two-sided enterprise as Christians created their identity in contact and exchange with others, and formulated responses to their neighbors of other faiths. The response was informed by the reality that the neighbor may have been a longtime friend or family member (as in the case of Paul's community at Corinth); the neighbor may have been a trading partner with whom the early Christians had professional relationships (as suggested in the encounters at Alexandria); the neighbor may have been the one who welcomed the stranger (as the story of Thomas envisions in its narrative). Embedded in distinct social locations, multiple elements must have gone into the formulation of a "Christian" response to the various persons of other faiths one might encounter. In these episodes, there is also a sense of the "others" whose perspectives one might attempt to hear. Recognizing the origins of many New Testament texts, the perspective of rabbis in local synagogues can be seen as they attempt to safeguard God's oneness and transcendence (affirmations from the Jewish tradition) in response to Christian claims about Jesus. In Paul's letter to the Corinthians, one hears the echoes of an invitation in the voice of the other that welcomed Christian neighbors to share a meal at their house of worship. The reader might even imagine their puzzlement over invitations rejected or second-guessed. Imagining Alexandria at the crossroads of Roman trade routes, the voices of tradespeople from Asia can be heard as they arrive and share their cultural and religious heritage in the process of everyday business transactions; and when Christian tradespeople traveled the Roman trade routes, encountering the other in his or her home country might require delicate concern for social and religious practices as good for business. In the fictional Acts of Thomas one early community envisioned the voice of the Indian other and imagined Christians responding to native peoples with care and concern. And so, as these episodes reveal, the Christian response to neighbors of other faiths have been responses of family disagreement, continued friendship, business partnership and care for the afflicted.

But the encounters of early Christians with religious difference are not all as positively creative as these episodes might suggest. As citizens of Rome, many Christians experienced their new Christian identity as a source of conflict with social and political power. As Jon Sobrino writes, "When Christianity began to spread through the empire, it came up against political religions that served to integrate and consolidate a people, to make myths about its origins and to glorify its history."[9] Such was the case with the cult of the emperor, where sacrifice was expected of all citizens as confirmation of allegiance and witness to the emperor's sacred nature. As simultaneously "Christian" and "citizen," individuals were caught in conflicting identities when they found themselves unable to maintain the practices expected of them as Roman citizens. Christians considered the cult of the emperor to compromise their affirmation of God's unique presence in Jesus Christ. Their non-Christian neighbors probably looked with suspicion on a cult that refused to show allegiance to the Empire and didn't hesitate to persecute Christians as scapegoats. As seen in the diary of one Christian woman named Perpetua, this conflict was also complicated by being not only citizen and Christian but the member of a Roman family as well. Despite the prominence of her family, Perpetua is jailed with her newborn son for refusing allegiance to the emperor. As recounted in her diary, the governor gives her the chance to show allegiance to the Empire, embrace her Roman citizenry and reject her Christian identity. Perpetua's claim to Christian identity and her refusal to participate in the cult of the emperor lands her among the wild beasts as entertainment for the governor's birthday. The encounter with religious difference in antiquity could quite possibly be a dangerous reality when one affirmed one's own distinctiveness. The voice of the other audible in this account is among the most heartbreaking as it reflects the reality that religious difference is not always far from home. Perpetua's father serves as a reminder that as Christians were developing a self-identity in contact and conversation with other faiths, they were also family members sharing deep connections across religious difference. There are traces of his voice in her diary as he pleads,

> Daughter...have pity on me your father, if I deserve to be called your father, if I have favoured you above all your brothers, if I have raised you to reach this prime of your life. Do not abandon me to be the reproach of men. Think of your brothers, think of your mother and your aunt, think of your child, who will not be able to live once you are gone. Give up your pride! You will destroy all of us![10]

Perpetua's refusal was not only treasonous to the Roman authorities but heartbreaking to her father as well. The conflicting elements of Perpetua's identity reflect the complexity of the response to religious difference when one recognizes that it is embedded in lived relationships, and not merely a theoretical exercise.

While Christians in real-life situations may have been creatively crafting responses to neighbors of diverse faiths, as Christianity organized into a more formal and institutional religion, theologians and spokespersons for the faith were crafting responses of their own. It is these that become systematized and established as *the* Christian response to religious difference; a response extracted from real-life contexts and centered on the issue of salvation. The early tradition that Jesus' salvific activity could be found among his followers continued as the community became organized into a more formal church. As the body of Christ, the church continued his salvific role in the world. But all too often, as theologians interpreted the tradition, the early sources became decontextualized, and salvation lost its specific connection to Jesus' healing activity and humble service. By the mid-third century, the saving role of the church became institutionalized and loss of salvation was used to threaten those who dissociated from the group. This transformation is clear in the example of Cyprian, bishop of Carthage (d. 258), who used the idea of salvation to encourage a return to the authority of the bishops. Warning so-called schismatics and heretics of the dangers of defying the institutionalizing church and its representatives, Cyprian writes,

Let them not think that the way of salvation exists for them, if they have refused to obey the bishops and priests.... The proud and insolent are killed with the sword of the Spirit, when they are cast out from the Church. For they cannot live outside, since there is only one house of God, and there can be no salvation for anyone except in the Church.[11]

What this third-century bishop used as a threat against those who would break from centralized authority was bequeathed to later Christians in the form of the axiom, *extra ecclesiam, nulla salus* — "outside the church, no salvation." While Cyprian directed his charge against other Christians and not toward persons of other faiths, it became a central teaching more widely applied to anyone not associated with the Christian church. In his reconstruction of this history entitled, *Salvation outside the Church? Tracing the History of the Catholic Response*, Francis Sullivan shows evidence of this in key statements that include council documents and papal proclamations. For example:

In 1215 Pope Innocent III and the Fourth Lateran Council stated, "There is one universal church of the faithful, outside of which no one at all is saved."

Pope Boniface VIII in his 1302 bull *Unam Sanctam* declared: "We are obliged by our faith to believe and to hold that there is one holy catholic and apostolic church; indeed, we firmly believe and sincerely confess this, and that outside of this church there is neither salvation nor the remission of sins.... Moreover, we declare, state and define that for every human creature it is a matter of strict necessity for salvation to be subject to the Roman Pontiff."

The 1442 Council of Florence proclaimed that: "[The Holy Roman Church] firmly believes, professes and teaches that none of those who exist outside of the Catholic Church — neither pagans nor Jews nor heretics nor schismatics — can become sharers of eternal life; rather they will go into the eternal fire 'which was prepared for the devil and his angels.' " (Matt. 25:42)

The Profession of Faith that emerged from the Council of Trent in 1564 summarizes and re-affirms the, "true Catholic faith, outside of which no one can be saved."[12]

When the axiom becomes the shorthand "official" response to neighbors of other faiths, salvation becomes less an existential reality engaged by practicing the art of following Christ's life and making real his kingdom-vision, and more the possession of an institutionalized church. As Sobrino writes,

> The reality of the Kingdom, including its finality, was transferred to the church, a transference that had something inevitable about it and could even have a certain legitimacy as long as the church worked for and became a sign of the Kingdom, but something that was also very dangerous... the church came to regard itself as the ultimate, not merely without duly stressing its differentiation from the Kingdom of God, but taking its place with a hubris inconceivable as coming from Jesus of Nazareth, conceiving itself *in principle* (whatever might have been its actual activities, holy or sinful) on the basis of power.[13]

The affirmations about Christ and salvation become transferred to affirmations about the body of the church. By the time of the colonial expansion of the fifteenth and sixteenth centuries, the axiom was taken to exclude all persons from salvation who were not explicitly Christian. The assumption was that all persons had the opportunity to join the Christian church and that if they chose instead to see the mystery of existence through other religions they were simply mistaken — and condemnably so. The official Christian response was to downplay God's incomprehensibility in favor of affirming the salvific role of the church. When missionaries of the colonial period found that the Christian message had not in fact reached the ends of the earth, and that countless cultures understood the mystery of existence in alternative ways, the result was an increase in the passionate efforts of missionaries to bring new peoples into the church.

But the efforts of missionaries did not take place in neutral settings. Quite the opposite was the case in the so-called "New World" when missionaries like Bartolomé de Las Casas encountered people of indigenous faiths in a complex theater intersected with political and economic forces. As Las Casas recounts, the Christianization of the Americas serves as representative of the rather un-Christian episodes in Christian history. In his *Devastation of the Indies* he writes,

> And the Christians, with their horses and swords and pikes began to carry out massacres and strange cruelties against them. They attacked the towns and spared neither the children nor the aged nor pregnant women nor women in childbed, not only stabbing them and dismembering them but cutting them to pieces as if dealing with sheep in the slaughter house. …They took infants from their mothers' breasts, snatching them by the legs and pitching them headfirst against the crags or snatched them by the arms and threw them into rivers, roaring with laughter and saying as the babies fell into the water, "Boil there, you offspring of the devil!" …They made some low wide gallows on which the hanged victim's feet almost touched the ground, stringing up their victims in lots of thirteen, in memory of Our Redeemer and His twelve Apostles, then set burning wood at their feet and thus burned them alive.[14]

The account Las Casas presents is rhetorically structured to demonstrate the perversion of Christianity which he saw in the actions of his Christian countrymen. The theological assertion "no salvation outside the church" rendered indigenous peoples "offsprings of the devil" and served as justification for murder.

But Las Casas's writings are unique in their attempt to chronicle the encounter from more than one perspective. He attempts to convey the experience also of native peoples. For example, in one episode, Hatuey, an Indian noble, alerts his people that the Christians are in close pursuit. He reminds them that his fellow noblemen have been put to death at Spanish hands and asks them, "Do you know why they do this?"

The Indians replied: "We do not know. But it may be that they are by nature wicked and cruel." And he told them: "No, they do not act only because of that but because they have a God they greatly worship and they want us to worship that God and that is why they struggle with us and subject us and kill us."

He had a basket full of gold and jewels and he said: "You see their God here, the God of the Christians. If you agree to it, let us dance for this God, who knows, it may please the God of the Christians and then they will do us no harm."[15]

Las Casas tells another story, this one of native resistance to conversion on the island of Cuba:

When tied to the stake, the cacique Hatuey was told by a Franciscan friar who was present, an artless rascal, something about the God of the Christians and of the articles of Faith. And he was told what he could do in the brief time that remained to him, in order to be saved and go to Heaven. The cacique, who had never heard any of this before, and was told he would go to the Inferno where, if he did not adopt the Christian Faith, he would suffer eternal torment, asked the Franciscan friar if Christians all went to Heaven. When told that they did he said he would prefer to go to Hell.[16]

From the perspective of native peoples, the actions of Christians made it very difficult to see any truth in Christianity, much less the fullness of salvific truth. Despite the unmatched material power wielded by Spanish Christians, Hatuey maintained the power of resistance that provides a counter-affirmation to those made by Christians through their word and action. Between the lines, the reader can hear Hatuey's counter-affirmation as one which rejects the lived reality of Christian patterns of action, rejecting also the Christian vision of salvation as it was made manifest in the Spanish Christians.

Through the voice of Hernando Pizarro (half-brother of Francisco Pizarro, conqueror of the Incas in Peru), we can hear the echo of native peoples much like those Las Casas tried to represent. While this episode reflects the historical reality that torture and threat of death were methods used to encourage native peoples to "convert" to Christianity, it also demonstrates the power of native faiths. As Pizarro recounts, "I had an old man tortured, who was one of the senior and intimate servants of their god. But he was so stubborn in his evil creed that I could never gather anything from him but that they really believed their devil to be a god."[17] Reading this entry against the grain, we hear the faint whisper of the other. Facing certain death at the hands of his religious others, this unnamed native priest maintained the power and agency to judge the affirmations being forced upon him under the cloak of conversion. The senior priest of the Incan religion was determined to defend the life-sustaining religious practices of his people, even under threat of torture and death. His resistance offers trace evidence of the counter-affirmations he embraced within his own native faith. At the edge of existence, threatened by torture and death, this priest assessed the affirmations of Spanish Christians (as they were presented to him) and those of his own faith tradition and chose to stand by the affirmations which he held to be true — those of his own native faith. "They really believed their devil to be a god," Pizarro writes incredulously. Indeed, the affirmation we can hear is that native peoples experienced their religious practices as putting them in touch with the mysterious reality of existence.

Seeing things from the perspective of people of other faiths complexifies also the history of Christian missions to the East. While the discourse of history often portrays the animosity and distance between Christians and persons of other faiths, in reality, there was a natural exchange and contact among those who visited cities on the Portuguese trade routes. A letter from Francis Xavier to his Jesuit companions in Rome, dated September 20, 1542, gives an example of this as he describes his stay on the island of Mozambique: "We remained on this island, which has a fortress of the king of Portugal, for six months. There are two towns on it, one of the Portuguese and the other of peaceful Moors." And again en route to Goa: "On our way we passed by Melinde, a city of peaceful Moors, where most of the time there are usually some Portuguese merchants." This same letter recounts an exchange between Xavier and a Muslim inhabitant of Melinde. He writes,

> One of the most distinguished Moors of this city of Melinde asked me to tell him whether the churches in which we are accustomed to pray are much frequented by us, and whether we are fervent in prayer, since, as he told me, they themselves had lost a great deal of their devotions, and he wished to know if the same had happened among the Christians; for in that city there are seventeen mosques but only three are being used, and only a very few attend them. Since he did not know the source of this loss of devotion, he was greatly confused. So great an evil, he told me could only have come from some great sin. After we had conversed for a long time, we still retained our own opinions. He was not satisfied when I told him that God our Lord, being most faithful in all his works, is not pleased with infidels and still less with their prayers; and this was the reason why God wanted their prayers to cease for he was not pleased by them.[18]

The casual nature of Xavier's description suggests that contact and conversation across religious difference was not altogether uncommon. Xavier had the opportunity to converse at length with a Muslim neighbor who appears to have taken Xavier as a dialogue partner in earnest. This unnamed, but "distinguished Moor" communicates his authentic concerns about the fluctuation in mosque attendance and piety among his fellow Muslims residing far from their native lands. Further, he seems to have seen patterns of religious lifestyle in common with the Christian Xavier, inquiring whether Christians experienced the same change in religious attendance in this new locale. But Xavier turns this point of connection back onto his conversation partner, and sadly, reveals the attitude of many Christians of his day: that the faith of his religious "others" was infidelity to God, and the destruction of alternative religious forms was pleasing to God. The affirmation of Christian relatedness to God becomes the sole site for relating to God, not only from the limited human perspective, but as Xavier claims, from God's perspective as well. He states quite boldly God's delights and disappointments as he argues that God "is not pleased with infidels and still less with their prayers." The eclipse of incomprehensibility in this case creates a God who is no longer the infinite mystery of the universe, but appears as a tribal ruler, interested only in the concerns of those of the Christian faith.

The same attitude predominates in Xavier's encounters with native Hindus during his work on India's soil. He sums up his theology of the religious other with the words, "The invocations of the pagans are hateful to God, since all their gods are devils."[19] With incomprehensibility erased by the certainty of knowing God's perspective, a theological distrust of native religious forms promoted a certain course of action which Xavier also describes in his letters:

> When they tell me about idolatries that are being practiced outside the villages, I collect all the boys of the village and go with them to the place where the idols have been erected; and the devil is more dishonored by the boys whom I take there than he is honored by their fathers and relatives when they made and worshipped them, for the boys take the idols and smash them to bits. They then spit upon them and trample them under their feet; and after this they do other things which, though it is better not to mention them by name, are a credit to the boys who do them against one who is so impudent as to have himself worshiped by their fathers.[20]

While not overpowering the people with a conquistador's army, Xavier's mission approach prefers the destruction of native religious forms in order to clear the space for Christianity. Such is the strength of affirmation when it eclipses incomprehensibility. Xavier holds no possibility that the native peoples of India and the visiting peoples of Islam might relate to the incomprehensible mystery of God in alternative ways. For Xavier, all that is not the Christian affirmation in Jesus Christ has its origin and end in the devil. Had the Christians of the Middle Ages held incomprehensibility in the forefront of their theological consideration of the encounter with people of other faiths, they might have heard more clearly the counter-affirmations of their native interlocutors. Xavier might have considered the alternative religious forms as native ways of relating to the mystery of God, and he might have heard the earnest concern of his Muslim conversation partner. As his letters reflect, affirmation trumps incomprehensibility, and Xavier cannot but reject any counter-affirmations held by people of other faiths.

While Xavier's letters provide insight into the chance encounters that could have taken place for missionaries to the east, it is not clear from them that he attempted long-term dialogue with the native peoples regarding their faith perspectives. The life of Roberto de Nobili represents a different approach. De Nobili so desperately wanted to converse with and convince the native peoples of India, that he set out to become neighbor to them, in a real sense. A generation after Xavier, de Nobili realized that chance encounters and outright rejection of native customs and religion was not providing the deep conversation that might lead to Christian conversions. He wanted to try a different strategy and set out to adapt himself to the cultural form of the native people, arguing, "The herald of the Gospel must himself, as far as possible, conform his way of acting to the social customs of these people."[21] Having approval from his superiors to attempt the experiment, de Nobili adopted the dress and style of the high caste Hindus. As Stephen Neill describes,

> It was by no means easy to carry out this design. He must wear only Indian dress — the long ochre robe of the *sannyasi,* with a second cloth cast over the shoulder. He must use only wooden sandals. He must eat only rice and vegetables, and be content with one meal a day.[22]

De Nobili learned Sanskrit, the language of the educated elite, and followed the rigid caste rules of Indian custom. In choosing the lifestyle of the sannyasi, de Nobili chose the occupation which was closest to his own vocation as a priest. Vincent Cronin explains, "Nobili discovered that the way of life most resembling that of a Christian priest was practised by a small group of men called sannyasis. The word was Sanskrit and meant 'one who resigns or abandons all.' ...Traditionally, it was the fourth and last stage of life recommended for brahmins.... [A sannyasi] wandered, living on alms, devoted to the contemplation of God and the problems of philosophy."[23] In adopting this lifestyle, he drew on the fact that brahmins were not only "religious-others" but shared in the similar contemplative state to which de Nobili and his companions had committed themselves. In the years de Nobili spent as a Christian sannyasi, his familiar appearance and ascetic lifestyle enabled him to meet Hindu brahmins who would inquire at his hermitage. Informed by his contact and friendship with learned brahmins, de Nobili engaged in religious exchange across Hindu-Christian lines. Such exchange is far different from the outright destruction of native forms employed by Xavier and others.

De Nobili drew from his actual exchanges to write texts in Tamil (the native language of his dialogue partners) designed to convince Hindus of the superior affirmations of Christianity. His works *Dialogue on Eternal Life* and *Inquiry into the Meaning of "God"* both reflect the way affirmation and incomprehensibility were considered, but not considerably balanced, in de Nobili's work. In both of these texts, de Nobili builds his argument on the overlap of Hindu and Christian discourses on the nature of reality and the nature of God. And although he follows Thomas Aquinas to admit God's incomprehensibility, the ultimate affirmation of Christian revelation seems to trump incomprehensibility and eliminate any possibility for distinctive Hindu perspectives on this mystery.

In his *Dialogue on Eternal Life,* de Nobili sets out an exchange between a fictional Christian master and inquiring native disciple. Representing the Hindu perspective, the disciple asks the master about the central concepts of the Christian faith concerning human knowledge of God. It is here that de Nobili reflects on God's incomprehensibility and demonstrates a continuity with the tradition of Aquinas. Notably, de Nobili insists that the human mind is incapable of fully knowing God: " . . . there are truths regarding the Lord which the human mind cannot contain."[24] To explain this incomprehensibility as "overabundance," de Nobili uses the metaphor of different sized pots, that is, while a big pot may contain a small pot within it, the human mind (being a pot of a certain capacity) cannot contain the mystery of God. For de Nobili, this means that certain truths can be attained by reason (those which can be contained in the human mind) and others can only be available through revelation.

This fictional account of the *Dialogue* likely draws from actual exchanges de Nobili himself experienced, suggesting that he had found agreement in certain aspects of the Hindu and Christian perspectives on God's incomprehensibility. Yet, instead of using the points of contact as sites for exploring the Hindu perspective, de Nobili clearly has in mind that the intersection should enable him to sway his interlocutors to the perspective of Christianity and rejection of Hindu views. When discussing revelation as providing insights into the mystery of God, de Nobili means only Christian revelation. After lengthy consideration of the incomprehensibility of God, de Nobili focuses his attention on the reasons why Hindu patterns of worshipping are not authentic but idolatrous. In his *Inquiry into the Meaning of "God,"* de Nobili devotes the entire text to demonstrating the characteristics of the true God and the ways Hindu Gods and Goddesses cannot represent truly the incomprehensible God.

De Nobili takes seriously the concept of the incomprehensibility of God, yet holds also the Christian affirmations about God to be true to the point of rejecting all counter-affirmations as they might be developed in the thought systems and experience of people of the Hindu faith. De Nobili scholars admit that his response to people of other faiths is limited because of his inability to genuinely consider the alternative perspective of his Hindu conversation partners. Yet, we might do what de Nobili did not by reading his accounts against the grain to recognize native people's reasoned preference for the affirmations of the Hindu faith. In spite of himself, de Nobili recounts such counter-affirmations. For example, in *Dialogue,* de Nobili has his fictional disciple represent a common Hindu affirmation, namely, "just as there are many roads leading to the same town and many rivers flowing into the same ocean, so too, they say, there are numerous viewpoints according to which one can know that transcendent-and-immanent Being and reach the ultimate bliss."[25] This belief might reflect the Hindu notion of the many incarnations and representations of the Ultimate Mystery in the various forms of Hindu Gods and Goddesses. The expression of multiplicity in the Deity has also been used by Hindus to argue for the multiplicity in the many forms of religion that might similarly lead to the ultimate

mystery. While de Nobili rejects this idea, his discourse nonetheless captures the indigenous perspective and offers contemporary
persons the possibility of recognizing the counter-affirmations from
this alternative faith perspective. A second example comes from a
letter de Nobili wrote in February 1609. Recalling a controversial
exchange between himself and local brahmins, he writes of the pro-
nouncement one brahmin brought against him and the teachings of
Christianity. De Nobili's letter recalls the voice of his native accuser,
who says to his fellow Hindus of de Nobili,

> See for yourselves, Brahmins, the stupidities uttered by this
> man [i.e., de Nobili]. He alone knows God; where then are
> those more learned scholars and doctors whom we held in
> such great honour because of their learning, who conducted so
> many famous disputations among us, whose disciples crowded
> our streets, whom so many sannyasis used to follow? Has this
> man alone the monopoly on salvation?[26]

Despite de Nobili's unique efforts to get to know his Hindu dialogue
partners by adopting their customs and living a sannyasi's lifestyle,
he nevertheless does not listen fully to the voice and perspective of
his religious other. As in his writings and the fictional exchanges
they present, the episode recounted in this letter shows that de Nobili fell short of listening to counter-affirmations about God. In this
letter, the voice of the other is captured when the native challenger
asks the pertinent question: Does de Nobili alone know God? De
Nobili has argued for God's incomprehensibility, but when dialoguing with Hindu scholars argues unique access to affirmations about
God through the Christian tradition alone. His interlocutor rightly
challenges the boundaries de Nobili places on affirmation and argues simply that the perspective of the learned scholars and doctors
of the native faith tradition be equally considered. Where knowledge of God in the Christian tradition has had its accompanying
claim of unique access to salvation, de Nobili's unnamed challenger
simply asks if Christianity has a monopoly on salvation. Hearing
the voice of the other in history, this unnamed brahmin's questions
remain relevant today. Recalling God's incomprehensibility as overabundance might suggest a possibility that de Nobili did not see —

that the faith traditions of India may offer alternative affirmations about the mysterious reality that Christians name "God."

While contemporary persons may want to move beyond de Nobili's limited perspective and listen more fully to the insights and affirmations of persons of other faiths, there is something to be learned from his approach. De Nobili recognized the commitment to living with and building relationships with persons of other faiths as a key strategy for encountering difference. Like de Nobili nearly five hundred years ago, there remains the need to get to know persons of other faiths by participating in their lifestyles and engaging with them day to day. In this approach to encounter, Matteo Ricci, a contemporary of de Nobili's, offers further patterns to follow. Like de Nobili, Ricci traveled the routes of exploration and trade to the Far East and held the conviction that if he could understand people's life practices and culture, he could more effectively dialogue on religious matters. Arriving in China, Ricci encountered the multiple religious forms of the land and attempted first to take on the role of a Buddhist monk. But, as Robert McClory writes, "since Confucianism was the official doctrine of China, Ricci soon decided he could make greater progress if he adopted the style and manner of a Confucian scholar. So he let his hair and beard grow and traded his Buddhist robes for the silk garments of the educated literati who studied the doctrines of the great master."[27] Spending years mastering the language and studying the classics of Confucius, Ricci identified overlaps in the religious systems of East and West. In his *The True Meaning of the Lord of Heaven*, Ricci specifically focuses on the nature of God in considering the commonalties, using the native phrase "Lord of Heaven" to indicate the one "whom our Western nations term Deus."[28] Notably, he sees the mysterious reality that Christians name "God" as the same reality identified in the Confucian system. Employing a natural theology, he insists that "the truth about the Lord of Heaven is already in the hearts of men."[29] And concludes that on this mysterious reality, Christianity and Confucianism agree, stating, "[Therefore] having leafed through a great number of ancient books, it is quite clear to me that the Sovereign on High and the Lord of Heaven are different only

in name."[30] Ricci's theological argument is premised on the overlap between the traditions of Confucianism and Christianity. But,
unlike de Nobili's use of commonalties to sway his readers away
from the native religious practices, Ricci engaged with the religious
forms of China, and accommodated some of the affirmations of
the other. He saw in Confucianism ideas similar to his own Christian view and considered even some of the non-Christian practices
as compatible with Christianity as it might be practiced in China.
Thus, Chinese converts to Christianity continued to practice an-
cestral rites honoring the dead and gave honor also to Confucius
himself. For these Chinese Christians, the affirmations of Christianity and those of Confucianism were not incompatible and could
be woven into a coherent vision and life practice. Yet, while Ricci
supported this interweaving of Christian and Confucian practices,
controversy ensued over whether indigenous religious forms could
be accommodated with Christianity. The debate lasted for decades.
As Douglas Lancashire and Peter Hu Kuo-chen report, "Finally, in
1704, the Roman Inquisition stated officially that Catholics were
forbidden to venerate the ancestors and Confucius, and could not
use the terms "Heaven" or "Sovereign on High" as names for
God."[31] As evidenced in the response from Rome, the official stance
toward other faiths was not as accommodating to alternative understandings of the mysterious, incomprehensible God that might
emerge from Chinese experience.

Taken together, the stories of Xavier, de Nobili and Ricci, and
the experience of those reflected in their writings, might inform the
encounter of religious others today. The first aspect to consider is
the way dialogue and exchange is rooted in the overlap of experience and points of contact between dialogue partners. In Xavier's
case, the unnamed Muslim who compares his faith community to
Xavier's demonstrates a recognition of the similarities that might
be sites of common experience and mutual understanding. While
Xavier rejects this opportunity for dialogue, people today might
keep their eyes open for those ways that life patterns and experience
overlap with those of neighbors of other faiths and provide contexts for conversation and mutual understanding. As both Ricci and
de Nobili found, fruitful conversation may not arise from merely

chance encounters with neighbors of other faiths, but from shared lifestyles and daily encounters. For twenty-first-century Christians in many parts of the world, this means welcoming the new immigrant families of other faiths as they join neighborhoods and become part of communities. It may also mean listening for the distinctiveness of religious outlooks among colleagues or members of the local community. Sharing in the daily practices of common lifestyles, opportunities emerge that are similar to those of de Nobili and Ricci five centuries ago. Understanding better the lifestyle and cultural practice of others provides a chance to see something of their perspective. But, when encountering the lifestyle and practice of the religiously other neighbor, cautionary lessons from the sixteenth century also arise. All too often, affirmation has eclipsed incomprehensibility, and Christians have been unable to hear the counter-affirmations of diverse religious perspectives. Recognizing this pattern, the path of Ricci (rather than de Nobili and Xavier) encourages the Christian to attempt to place what is learned about the other's faith perspective into the larger context of the incomprehensible mystery of God. We might consider the possibility of diverse practices and perspectives offering distinctive ways of experiencing and responding to this overabundant yet mysterious reality.

The patterns of eclipsing incomprehensibility and turning a deaf ear to counter-affirmations was representative not only of the encounters of the sixteenth century, but continued into the eighteenth, nineteenth and twentieth centuries. And in contrast to de Nobili's and Ricci's respect for indigenous cultures, the missions established in this time period often sought the cultural as well as religious transformation of native peoples. What this meant was that conversion to Christianity was attended by radical changes in social patterns. In African mission contexts, for example, polygamy was often seen as contrary to Christianity and thus male converts were required to break ties with all wives but one. This often left previously married women with no financial or social support in a culture tied very much to family networks. Other new Christians were encouraged to renounce their ties with family since these ties would connect them to the traditional African forms of social and religious observance. Indeed, many missionaries encouraged converts to leave the tribal community as evidence of their loyalty to Christ. Breaking ties with their families and cultural forms, converts were baptized with Western names and converted their style of dress to that of the Western missionaries. The definition of what was "Christian" became conflated with specific European cultural forms. For example, Elizabeth Lees Price (missionary and sister-in-law of David Livingstone) tried to convince her African companions that "in civilized and especially Christian countries a slender figure is admired, unlike the fat African model, because it is thought a dishonor to eat too much. The more civilized and more Christ-like the Bakwena became, the more they would admire slenderness and not fatness."[32] As evidenced in the writings of missionaries of this time, many Western Christians adopted the attitude that Africans needed to be reshaped, reclothed, renamed, and often remarried, all according to Western standards of the day.[33]

Evidenced in these examples are the attitudes of cultural superiority which intertwined with religious and moral superiority in the workings of many missions. As the missions were often associated with colonial political order, these multiple sources for attitudes of superiority worked together. Thus, the missionary aims of conversion and colonial aims of advancing European civilization (through cultural and commercial success) were often "interwoven into a single project."[34] Missionary efforts in colonial systems were often understood as projects that could "civilize and control" native peoples by bringing them to the "higher" forms of Western culture and religion, thus easing European ability to govern in colonial contexts.[35] In government circles, the writings of religious encounter produced by the missionaries were appreciated as a means by which to understand and thus adapt to and control colonial subjects. So widespread was the attitude that missionary activity had a civilizing function that colonial governments withdrew support from those missions which seemed to upset the colonial "civilized" order;[36] and missionaries denied the requests for baptism of native peoples deemed insufficiently civilized, as was the case in Aboriginal Australia.[37] The Christian encounter with religious others was steeped in attitudes of cultural and religious superiority and these had material effects. As John Hick explains,

> the moral validation of the imperial enterprise rested upon the conviction that it was a great civilizing and uplifting mission, one of whose tasks was to draw the unfortunate heathen up into the higher, indeed highest, religion of Christianity. Accordingly the gospel played a vital role in the self-justification of Western imperialism. . . . In the eighteenth and nineteenth centuries the conviction of the decisive superiority of Christianity infused the imperial expansion of the West with a powerful moral impetus and an effective religious validation without which the enterprise might well not have been psychologically viable.[38]

With the focused aim of bringing the "natives" into the superior cultural and religious forms, conversion efforts continued with vigor in colonial settings. But the writings of missionaries tend to gloss over resistance to conversion, because home congregations would have been far more interested in the "successes." In resisting conversion to Christianity, native peoples insist on the reality of God and salvation made available to them through their native religious forms. Captured in the texts of history is the reaction of missionaries whose efforts are thwarted by the agencies of indigenous peoples. For example, *The Missionary Register,* produced by the Church Missionary Society, reprints an 1818 sermon by Archdeacon Potts, whose work in India was tested by native peoples. His sermon reads,

> If you urge them with their gross and unworthy misconceptions of the nature and the will of God, or the monstrous follies of their fabulous theology, they will turn it off with a *sly civility* perhaps, or with a popular and careless proverb. You may be told that "heaven is a wide place, and has a thousand gates"; and that their religion is one by which they hope to enter.[39]

Here again is the response of native peoples to the claims and affirmations of Christian missionaries. From the perspective of Western Christians, the native faiths were "unworthy misconceptions" about

God. Clearly, the Christian affirmations about God eclipsed God's incomprehensibility and overabundance, and the possibility that diverse conceptions about this mystery could be sustained. Yet, in this Christian reflection, the voice of the native other is also present. The anonymous "other" argues for multiple affirmations about the mysterious reality that Christians name "God" in the claim that "heaven is a wide place and has a thousand gates." Here is overabundance seen from the perspective of the other. And while Christians of the nineteenth century, like Archdeacon Potts, may have rejected the possibility that the native religious forms provide access to the mysterious reality of God, Christians of the twenty-first century might reconsider. Hearing the voice of the other in history, Christians are offered a new way to construct a response to religious difference.

By considering past encounters from the perspective of Christians and their "others," insights for current responses are made available. The simplest insight is that encounter and engagement with persons of diverse faiths can be seen as part of what it means to be "Christian." From the earliest Christians sharing life practices with Jews and Greeks in antiquity, to sixteenth-century projects in which Christians were embedded in the lives of Hindus and Confucians, to contemporary cities where Christians live alongside religious others, discussion and dialogue have long been part of Christian practice. Christians have joined in meals and shared lifestyles with neighbors of other faiths which has allowed for conversation and exchange to develop in ongoing contact. For many Christians, their identity as Christian was developed in these conversations with people of other faiths. But the deeper insight here is that meeting the "religious other" is never just a meeting of religious others, but is embedded in social contexts where persons are informed by a diversity of concerns and a multiplicity of identities. Some of these identities are shared — like being the member of the same family, citizen of the same locale, or follower of a similar lifestyle; others of these identities are distinctive — as is specifically the case with religious identities in the meeting. Furthermore, these episodes have shown that embedding in social contexts means that religious responses have material consequences. One set of material consequences comes in the powerful memory of Christian care for the non-Christian neighbor and the reciprocal care shown by the native people of various lands. In the Acts of Thomas for example, Thomas's primary encounter with the native peoples of India was in the care and concern he demonstrated for the poor. In other episodes, Thomas is welcomed by native peoples who hear his distinctive religious message. This welcome by the peoples of India is repeated in the historical accounts of Roberto de Nobili who was able to converse with the native peoples because of their openness to his presence among them. Matteo Ricci also was often welcomed as a stranger by members of the Confucian elite in China. Christian care for the non-Christian other is evident also in the life of Bartolomé de Las Casas, who saw it as his Christian mission to defend the humanity of the native peoples against the dehumanization brought on by his own Christian compatriots. The powerful memory of reciprocal care has its flip side in the dangerous memory of religious encounters intertwined with social, political and material gain. Eclipsing incomprehensibility, the conquerors of Latin America employed Christian affirmations as an excuse for horrific actions that destroyed native peoples and claimed native land and goods as their own. The incomprehensibility of God was again eclipsed by modern certainties about the progression of human culture and human relatedness to God. In degrading diverse religious and cultural forms in the attempt to "convert and civilize" colonized peoples, Christian affirmations have indeed served the material and social gain of Christians well into the twentieth century.

This look into history has also tried to learn from the perspective of religious "others" in the texts of history. The powerful voice of the Hindu brahmin who asked de Nobili whether he alone knows God and if he alone has a monopoly on salvation was one such example. The bold statements of faith of native peoples who refused conversion — even under threat of death — preferring their own religious forms to those they saw demonstrated by Christians, is another example. Reading Christian history against the grain recognizes the equal force of counter-affirmations as persons of different faiths meet against the backdrop of ultimate mystery. Maintaining the agency and respecting the experience of the "other," Christians are encouraged to reconsider the mysterious reality of "God" as it might be seen from the other's perspective.

Through the lens of history and with the help of a variety of perspectives, these important insights can shape a contemporary response to persons of other faiths. But today's is not the first modern generation to attempt the theological reflection that can serve as a framework for this encounter. In fact, in the last half of the twentieth century, numerous Christian theologians have taken up the challenge of understanding religious difference through the lens of Christian faith. As I, too, am seeking such a theological understanding, the following chapter will investigate those earlier projects to see what additional resources are available and what contemporary conceptual pitfalls there are to avoid.

Chapter Three

THE IMPASSE OF
SAMENESS OR DIFFERENCE

IT IS CLEAR FROM HISTORY that Christians have long been in contact and conversation with people of other faiths. In fact, Christian identity has often been informed by such meetings. A person's self-understanding and worldview are articulated ever more clearly in distinction to the alternatives. At the same time, Christians have often learned from other faiths or seen some similarities between their Christian perspective and that of others. It is also clear that these encounters have at least two sides and that people of other faiths have simultaneously made claims about the nature of existence. The voice of the other in history has raised some potent theological questions. Considering the diverse religions through the lens of Christian faith, perhaps no questions are as powerful as those spoken by an unnamed Hindu brahmin of seventeenth-century India when he challenged the Christian mission of Roberto de Nobili. He asked, "Does this man alone know God? Does he alone have the monopoly on salvation?" Defending his native religious insights and understandings about the incomprehensible mystery of existence, de Nobili's interlocutor challenged him to consider alternative perspectives. Some four hundred years later, Christians are challenged still by these questions. Presented directly, the question is: do theological constructions presuppose that Christians alone know God and that Christians alone have a monopoly on salvation? As seen in the course of Christian history, the answer has often been simply — "yes." That is, an exclusivist point of view has reigned in which Christian affirmations have been defended as the only route to knowledge of God and salvation. But in the late twentieth and early twenty-first centuries, increasingly Christians have reconsidered such an exclusivist point of view. Defending the universality of God, Christian theology has moved in new directions while maintaining the critical elements of God's incomprehensibility and affirmations about God in the person of Jesus of Nazareth. As this chapter explores how this has been done, the reader may recall the three requisites for a theology of religious pluralism laid out in chapter 1. First, for a theology of religions to be useful in connecting with people of other faiths, it needs to offer strategies for communication across difference. Second, for it to be in continuity with the tradition, it must provide ways of maintaining what has been affirmed about God through the person of Jesus. And third, in order for a theology to have positive impact in lived situations, it must be attentive to the material consequences it holds for practice. With these criteria in mind, the contemporary theological positions of exclusivism, inclusivism, pluralism, and particularism will be assessed with an eye to their usefulness for current encounters across religious difference.

The exclusivist thinking that has reigned throughout Christian history rests on a deep gulf between Christians and people of other faiths. Those who follow the diverse religious traditions are categorically different from Christians, and knowledge of God and salvation are the distinct possession of Christianity. As one might guess, the exclusivist thought pattern often sustains negative courses of action. It was exclusivism that encouraged Francis Xavier to destroy the sacred objects of native peoples in India and to close off conversation with the Muslim whom he met. It was exclusivism that drove the Spanish quest for an expanded Christendom and that tolerated the destruction of native peoples as consistent with God's plan. It was also exclusivism that encouraged missionaries in Africa and India to westernize their converts, all but eliminating native cultural forms in the process. Theologians today are increasingly aware of the dangerous memory of earlier responses to religious difference. Taking the other seriously means also taking responsibility for the negative impact of past theological thinking and trying to present new ways of thinking that move beyond exclusivist tendencies and their material outcomes.

But exclusivism has also been used as a stance against the horrors of history. For example, Karl Barth's work is decidedly exclusivist, with access to God solely through Jesus Christ. Barth's exclusivism rests on the infinite qualitative distinction between God and humanity and the singular bridge between them: Jesus Christ. As Barth writes, "Therefore, to know God in His Word means primarily and comprehensively to know Him Himself. He Himself stands before man, and He Himself is either known in this way or He is not known at all."[1] When Barth refers to "God's Word" he means the revelation of God in Jesus of Nazareth. Knowledge of God comes exclusively through the way God has made Godself known in Jesus Christ. And while Jesus' disciples knew God's Word by following Jesus, centuries of Christians down through the ages have knowledge of God mediated through the Word of God in Christian Scripture. This exclusivism limits knowledge of God to Christian sources and, for Barth, "...without the knowledge of God there is no salvation."[2] It seems that, for Barth, Christians alone have the monopoly on salvation. Yet, Barth's exclusivism served as a prophetic voice against those who would claim knowledge of God in ways that ran contrary to the life-giving practice of Jesus of Nazareth. Writing in Hitler's Germany, Barth affirmed God's design in the uniqueness of Jesus Christ and the witness of Christian scripture as a way to stand against the dehumanizing powers of this world. In his own social context, there were innumerable Christians who followed the life-destructive patterns of Hitler's regime. While an effective tool against dehumanizing actions within Christian nations, Barth's exclusivism translates also into a rejection of other religions. In fact, he writes at length about the way religion is a human product which bears no fruit, while revelation — available exclusively in the action of God in Jesus Christ — brings salvation.[3] The theological stance of exclusivism leaves little room for real conversation with neighbors of other faiths.

In the last half of the twentieth century, theologians have been especially interested in moving beyond the exclusivist heritage of Christianity and articulating new theologies of religious pluralism increasingly sensitive to persons of other faiths. But not all Christian communities are willing to let go of the exclusivist claims as they appear in the New Testament. As Roger Haight notes, "[exclusivism] is usually identified with conservative evangelical Christians who read a number of New Testament texts in a literal way."[4] While exclusivism has fallen out of favor in mainstream theological thinking, it still thrives as a theological response to religious difference. Furthermore, even in Christian groups that acknowledge the human hand in the writing of scripture and read the text in nonliteral ways, it is not always easy to eliminate the exclusivist tendencies within the tradition. In fact, many Christians would say that to do so would erase the particularity of Christianity altogether. The pull toward exclusivism remains as Christian theologians attempt to safeguard the distinctiveness of Christian faith affirmations about God's unique work in Jesus Christ. And so, while contemporary thought moves increasingly away from exclusivist stances, there is always a counter-pull toward defending Jesus' unique role in bringing salvation to humanity.

The exclusivist protection of tradition can be seen even as theological arguments move in new directions. For example, in the magisterium of the Catholic Church exclusivism has been decidedly rejected. It is no longer the case that the teaching authority requires assent to the axiom, "no salvation outside the church" as it has in previous eras. And yet, when recent texts have been written to respond to the reality of religious diversity, there is trace evidence of exclusivist patterns of thinking. For example, when the Congregation for the Doctrine of the Faith issued the document *Dominus Iesus,* the argument was not exclusivistic, but the tone of the document often tended to be. The document rearticulates the statements of the Catholic faith,

> . . . according to which the full and complete revelation of the salvific mystery of God is given in Jesus Christ. Therefore, the words, deed, and entire historical event of Jesus, though limited as human realities, have nevertheless the divine Person of the Incarnate Word, "true God and true man" as their subject. For this reason, they possess in themselves the definitiveness

and completeness of the revelation of God's salvific ways, even
if the depth of the divine mystery in itself remains transcendent
and inexhaustible.[5]

Here, incomprehensibility and affirmation stand together: the text
affirms God's "mystery" and "inexhaustibility"; nevertheless, on
the basis of Catholic faith affirmations, the document claims knowledge of God's activity in that Christianity retains the definitive and
complete revelation of salvation. The document stands firmly by the
affirmation that the "fullness of salvation" is found in the Catholic
Church, while other persons are "in a gravely deficient situation" —
"objectively speaking."[6] Here, exclusivist tendencies so thoroughly
promote Christian affirmations that they eclipse incomprehensibility. Exclusivist patterns claim a "God's-eye view" that serves as a
basis for making "objective" judgments about the negative status
of persons of other faiths.

The outcome of exclusivist thinking today may have the same
repercussions that it has had throughout history. Someone who
holds an exclusivist position need not listen to nor learn from his/her
neighbor of another faith. After all, if you have already judged the
other's position to be incorrect, why engage in the conversation?
(Unless, of course, to convince the person of his/her error.) While exclusivists may still engage with people of other faiths for the express
purpose of conversion, there is no genuine dialogue. The exclusivist
does not see the perspective of the other as possibly an alternative
view of God's overabundant mystery.

It is an exclusivist attitude that underlies many of the religious
hate crimes witnessed even in the last fifteen years in America and
abroad. Keep in mind that an exclusivist stance alone does not lead
to destructive actions; however, an exclusivist attitude can encourage the antagonism at the root of these offenses. In her book, *A
New Religious America: How a "Christian Country" Has Become
the World's Most Religiously Diverse Nation*, Diana Eck chron-
icles some religiously motivated hate crimes which seem to stem
from exclusivist attitudes. She witnesses Buddhist temples dese-
crated by vandals who left hate-filled messages in spray paint on
the walls. She recounts how Hindus and Sikhs have been attacked

and beaten to death when religious difference becomes a visible marker and target for antiforeign sentiment. The book also brings to light the nonviolent discrimination that has occurred when numerous communities across the country have attempted to exclude non-Christian congregations and block the creation of houses of worship in their locales. Eck gives a particularly telling example:

> When Muslims in Edmond, the suburb of Oklahoma City where the University Central of Oklahoma is located, planned to build a mosque in 1992, a move was made to deny a building permit because, as a Pluralism Project researcher reported, "One of the minister's wives [sic] attended the first public hearing and vehemently opposed it. She said, 'The constitution says One nation under God, and that's a Christian God. These people have no right to be here.' "[7]

The unnamed minister's wife voices what may be under the surface of many exclusionary practices toward people of other faiths, that is, that the Christian affirmations about God mean that God is exclusively "a Christian God." From a theological perspective this runs counter to the tradition that identifies God as the source of *all* existence and creator of all humanity. It is also an eclipse of incomprehensibility that has material outcomes for the Muslims who live in the community. The exclusion from relatedness to God also becomes an exclusion from the social community and political process, as the woman claims that the Muslim community has "no right to be here." Even in the twentieth century, even in our own backyards, exclusivist attitudes have material consequences in the lives of actual people.

In exclusivist theologies and those that employ language that leans in an exclusivist direction, the classic stance does what it has done throughout history — incomprehensibility is eclipsed by affirmation. The certainty of one's own understanding of the mystery of God seems to just about erase that mystery. This leaves little room for growth or learning something new from the perspective of other faiths. *Dominus Iesus'* designation of non-Catholics as being in a "gravely deficient situation" demonstrates the implications of certainty — all other perspectives and persons are evaluated as "less than" those of the Roman Catholic Church. Designating this evaluation as "objective" seems to assert a God's eye view that justifies this negative judgment. The examples of hate crimes and sentiments discriminating against religious "others" are reminders that theological stances have material implications as they are embedded in lived situations. Exclusivism does not leave much room for following the pattern of healing care demonstrated by Jesus in the New Testament, nor does it allow for real conversation; and perhaps most importantly, it seems to eclipse the incomprehensibility of God. This stance glosses over the fact that while the tradition includes affirmations about the definitive action of God in Jesus Christ, it also contains the lines of scripture that ask, "Who has known the mind of the Lord?" (Rom. 11:34; Isa. 40:13). Christians are challenged to hold together affirmations about God in Jesus *and* the ultimate incomprehensibility of God.

By the middle of the twentieth century in mainstream theological circles, the dangers of exclusivism and its inability to hold together affirmation and incomprehensibility were widely recognized. A shift began toward inclusivist theological thinking. If the reader recalls the questions of de Nobili's brahmin, he or she can see the difference between exclusivism and inclusivism more clearly. Recall the questions: Do Christians alone know God? Do Christians have the monopoly on salvation? In response, the exclusivist answers "yes"; while the inclusivist offers a cautionary "not exactly." Like exclusivism, inclusivism identifies Jesus Christ as the unique mediator of salvation. Yet, inclusivism also underscores God's universality and affirms that God desires the salvation of all people, asserting that salvation takes place through Jesus Christ, even for persons who don't know Jesus Christ. People of other faiths are "included" in the salvation that Jesus Christ makes available. In relation to scriptural sources, one might say that inclusivists aim to hold in tension the two faith affirmations of 1 Timothy, which reads:

[God our Savior] desires everyone to be saved and to come to the knowledge of truth. For there is one God; there is also one mediator between God and humankind, Christ Jesus.... (1 Tim. 2:4–5)

The passage affirms that when Christians employ the term "God" they are not referring to "a Christian God" as if God stood as the tribal leader of Christians alone. Rather, the letter assumes that when Christians use the term "God" they are referring to the one mysterious source and end of all existence. This universality is an element exclusivists often overlook. For inclusivists, God desires the most complete end for all humanity, that is, that all will be saved. But the passage also reveals the essential element retained by inclusivist Christian thought, namely, that while God wills the salvation of all peoples, salvation itself comes through Jesus Christ alone. People of other faiths can participate in the salvation Christ makes possible, but it is uniquely Jesus Christ who makes salvation a reality.

This argument often draws on incomprehensibility as a way to say that non-Christians are included in the salvation of Jesus Christ even if we cannot explain how. For example, *Dominus Iesus* affirms that "the salvific action of Jesus Christ, with and through his Spirit, extends beyond the visible boundaries of the Church to all humanity."[8] It is important to note that while salvation is available outside the church, this salvation is made available through Jesus Christ and his Spirit. How this happens is part of the divine mystery. Quoting *Gaudium et Spes* from the Second Vatican Council, the text of *Dominus Iesus* asserts that "all men and women who are saved share, though differently, in the same mystery of salvation in Jesus Christ through his Spirit."[9] Incomprehensibility is invoked to explain how non-Christians participate in the salvation of Jesus Christ.

While many contemporary theologies hold an inclusivist stance, the work of Karl Rahner is truly exemplary of this theological position. When Rahner wrote in the middle of the twentieth century, as a Jesuit, Roman Catholic priest, he was concerned to safeguard the traditional theological affirmations while opening a space for accepting non-Christian religions. He held together the two classic doctrines: God's universal will for salvation and Jesus Christ as the unique mediator. But rather than start with the doctrines themselves, Rahner tried to explain Christian theology by rooting it in experiences common to all human beings. A closer look at his theology will help sketch the theological nuances of inclusivism.

Rahner begins with the fundamental experience of human growth that can be seen in the processes of knowing, making free choices and loving. These are the characteristic events that make human beings human. But they also are gateways for recognizing the incomprehensible mystery of God. As Rahner explains, each and every time the human person goes outside him or herself in growth or love, or extends into the unknown in the process of knowing, or pursues a life choice not bound by the logic of our material world, that individual extends beyond the limits of what he or she presently is and creates something new. These processes of growth take place in all human beings, without exception. And when humans participate in growth and transcendence, they are reaching out toward the one who created them, the one whom Christians name "God." In creating human beings, God communicates to each individual and propels the ongoing transcendence that is the hallmark of human existence. As Rahner argues, this self-communication of God takes place "always and everywhere and to every person as the innermost center of his[her] existence."[10] As the human person participates in life and the ongoing process of growth, he or she is capable of recognizing that the dynamism of transcendence is sustained by God's indwelling in human nature.[11] As Rahner writes, "deep in our own nature God dwells."[12] At the same time, these processes bring human beings to an encounter with the infinite horizon of transcendence, the holy mystery of God. By focusing on human experiences of growth and identifying God as both source and goal of transcendence, Rahner establishes the universality of God's presence to all people.

When human beings are open to their own growth, they are accepting God's self-communication of grace. Here is where Rahner introduces the idea of salvation. Since growth and transcendence constitute the human response to the God who created them, communion with God is begun through the process of transcendence in this life and fulfilled beyond the boundaries of our material world. "Salvation" is understood as the fullness of human becoming and the culmination of the process of transcendence. Rahner writes,

"Anyone who does not close him [or her] self to God in an ultimate act of his [or her] life...this person finds salvation."[13] Just as it is evident that people of all faiths participate in growth and transcendence, Christians can trust that non-Christians also can experience the fullness of this process in salvation. This is regardless of the religious tradition to which they belong. Rahner concludes, "As God's real self-communication in grace, therefore, the history of salvation and revelation is coexistent and coextensive with the history of the world and of the human spirit, and hence also with the history of religion."[14] Rahner offers a positive valuation of the diversity of religions in that God's self-communication or "revelation" is not limited to the explicitly Christian witness. He allows for the possibility that the diversity of religions may be contexts for and expressions of the human encounter with God in history.

So far, the first affirmation of inclusivist theology is evident: God is a universal reality for all humanity and all humanity can accept God's universal invitation to salvation. Yet, inclusivism also identifies Jesus Christ as the unique mediator of God's salvation. Holding both of these affirmations together, Rahner must explain *why* Jesus is the unique mediator of salvation, especially for persons of the diverse religions of the world. In Rahner's explanation, in order for transcendence to be available to all humanity, it must have been made a reality by the perfect human being. The indwelling that propels human transcendence was activated precisely when God's self-communication was received in perfect human acceptance. Searching history to find the one in whom God's self-communication was made complete, the Christian finds Jesus Christ.[15] Christians find in Jesus Christ, the one who was fully open to the mystery of God, whose self-consciousness was consciousness of the human participation in God. Through the eyes of Christian faith, the perfection of human growth and transcendence was made real in Jesus Christ. Perfecting the structure of human being in the world, Christ becomes "the very thing towards which [hu]mankind is moving."[16] The witness of Jesus reveals to humanity its fundamental connectedness and dynamism toward God. But more than mere witness, Christ's acceptance of God's self-communication stamps the rest of humanity with the possibility of transcending toward God. Therefore, "the achievement by any man of his proper and definitive salvation is dependent upon Jesus Christ."[17]

While human relationships with God are as diverse as the specific locations that sustain the process of human becoming, they are, as Rahner understands them, "basically the same" in that they rest on the perfect humanity of Jesus Christ. As he explains, "The relationship of God to man is basically the same for all [humanity], because it rests on the Incarnation, death and resurrection of the one Word of God made flesh."[18] All those who follow Christ's path of accepting the self-communication of God achieve "salvation in the proper and Christian sense of God's absolute self-communication in absolute closeness, and hence it also means what we call the beatific vision."[19] What is important to recognize here is that, in Rahner's understanding, persons can follow Christ's path of accepting the self-communication of God (in the growth of knowledge, will and love), even without realizing that it is Christ who has made this transcendence possible. Just as Christ constitutes salvation for Christians, so too does Christ constitute the salvation of all persons. In Rahner's own words, " ... anyone who has let himself be taken hold of by this grace can be called with every right an 'anonymous Christian.' "[20] This is Rahner's famous phrase and it encapsulates the theological stance of inclusivists. All persons have the possibility for God's salvation through Jesus Christ whether they know it or not. Those who participate "anonymously" in the process made possible by Jesus are destined for salvation as "anonymous Christians." A key element in the identification of persons as "anonymous Christians" is that while they may be found in other traditions, they have a mysterious connection with Christ. That is, it is Christ *within* the other religions that propels the anonymous Christian's dynamism toward God. The diverse faith traditions might serve as positive contexts in which to encounter Christ, and may be implicit expressions of that encounter, but that which is salvific in the religions is the result of Christ anonymously present there.

Rahner's inclusivism reflects today's mainstream theological position, and might be assessed on the criteria outlined in the opening of this chapter. That is, how is inclusivism useful in connecting with people of other faiths? How is it in continuity with the tradition? And what are the implications for practice that this approach entails? Inclusivism stands in continuity with the tradition as it affirms Jesus' role as mediator of God's salvation, and even includes a measure of God's incomprehensibility since how Christ is present in other religions remains somewhat of a mystery. As a positive step away from exclusivism, inclusivism does not require that Christians reject other religions, since these can potentially be vehicles for the salvific presence of Jesus Christ. This affords an openness to other religious traditions that exclusivism does not. But the inclusivist position of Karl Rahner does not really allow for conversation that hears the distinctive affirmations of our religiously other neighbors. It seems as though Christians know in advance what to expect in the faith perspectives of other religions because they are looking for "Christ" present there. This theology promotes a search for sameness that ignores the distinctive affirmations that might be found in the lives and experiences of persons of other faiths.

While Rahner's is the most explicit search for sameness that eliminates the counter-affirmations of people of other faiths, more recent Spirit Christologies echo his position. For example, Jacques Dupuis in *Toward a Christian Theology of Religious Pluralism* uses Rahner's model in articulating a vision of the many paths of diverse religions that lead ultimately to the salvation constituted by Jesus Christ. Dupuis explains that "the person of Jesus Christ and the Christ-event are 'constitutive' of salvation of the whole of humankind; in particular, the event of his death-resurrection opens access to God for all human beings, independently of their historical situation."[21] A Trinitarian theology of religions enables Dupuis to envision the presence of Christ in the diversity of religions.[22] Similarly, Gavin D'Costa's Christocentric Trinitarian theology is indebted to Rahner. Holding the revelation of God in Christ as normative, D'Costa's inclusivism "facilitates an openness to the world religions, for the activity of the Spirit cannot be confined to Christianity."[23] Many Trinitarian theologies of religious pluralism are similarly indebted to Rahner's inclusivism, seeing Christ present in other religions through the workings of the Holy Spirit.[24] While moving in a more pluralistic direction, the Logos-centered process

theology of John Cobb[25] and the universal Christ principle in Raimon Panikkar's work[26] also tend toward the inclusivist sameness
that is the hallmark of Rahner's thinking.[27] In each of these inclusivist theological projects, God's universality and even mystery are
maintained, as is the affirmation of knowability of God through
Jesus Christ. What is missing in the inclusivist position is the genuine openness to the distinctiveness of others' affirmations about
God. To the inclusivist theologian, we ask again what was asked
of Roberto de Nobili in the seventeenth century: Do Christians
alone know God? While opening a space for encountering persons
of other faiths, the inclusivist position privileges the Christian tradition as the path to salvation and Christian affirmations as what
humans can know of God.

Whereas those Spirit Christologies which follow Rahner's lead
are likely candidates for seeking sameness in other religions and
maintaining Christian affirmations as the norm for understanding
God, many of the so-called pluralist positions seek sameness and
privilege Christian affirmation as well, albeit implicitly. The pluralist position moves away from both exclusivism and inclusivism
to affirm that there are multiple ways to God and that Christians
do not have a monopoly on salvation. Indeed, in chapter 2 it was
a pluralist who asserted, "just as there are many roads leading to
the same town and many rivers flowing into the same ocean, so
too, they say, there are numerous viewpoints according to which
one can know that transcendent-and-immanent Being and reach
the ultimate bliss."[28] It was also a pluralist who asserted, "heaven
is a wide place, and has a thousand gates"[29] with various religions
leading to the same salvation. These historical voices are echoed
by the pluralists of today who hold that the mysterious reality that
Christians name "God" is encountered through the various religious traditions of the world. This approach respects the different
paths of diverse religions as equally valid responses to the mystery
of God. Yet, while affirming the universality of God, too often the
pluralist rests this affirmation on a perceived similarity among all
religions. The distinctiveness or difference of the other is minimized
in order to capitalize on the sameness. The pluralist position encourages people to look for the sameness in their religiously other

neighbor, but what happens when differences persist instead? Does the pluralist position leave room for listening to and learning from the counter-affirmations of diverse faith perspectives in a way that opens up new understandings of the mysterious reality of God?

Take the classic pluralist expression of John Hick as an example. Fundamental to his project is the idea of the incomprehensibility of God, for which Hick employs the notion of God as "the Transcendent" — beyond human access and understanding. Hick describes God as "ineffable," that is, "having a nature that is beyond the scope of our networks of human concepts."[30] With God's incomprehensibility established, Hick wonders about the religious expressions of the diverse world religions and whether they relate to this incomprehensible God. He argues that the ineffable reality of God is experienced through the different human concepts of the various traditions. The way we can know that they are all experiencing the same reality is that every religious tradition (in Hick's explanation) promotes a turn "from self-centeredness to Reality-centeredness."[31] Hick explains how Jesus Christ promotes the turn from selfishness to care for the other and relatedness to God, and then looks to each of the "great world religions" for a similar idea. Of the traditions Hick asserts,

> They all teach the ideal of seeking the good of others as much as of oneself. For example, from Buddhism, "As a mother cares for her son, all her days, so towards all living things a man's mind should be all-embracing"; from Hinduism, "One should never do that to another which one regards as injurious to one's own self. This, in brief, is the rule of Righteousness"; from Confucianism, "Do not do to others what you would not like yourself"; from Taoism, the good man "will regard [others'] gains as if they were his own, and their losses in the same way"; from Christianity, "As ye would that men should do to you, do ye also to them likewise"; from Judaism, "What is hateful to yourself do not do to your fellow man. This is the whole of the Torah"; and from Islam, "No man is a true believer unless he desires for his brother that which he desires for himself."[32]

Hick has carefully sifted through the various elements of each religious tradition to identify a sameness within. Finding this similarity among them, Hick concludes that each of the great world religions is a response to the ineffable mystery that Christians name "God."

The pluralists make powerful statements about what might bind together persons of diverse religious traditions. When people witness a similarity between their own religious practices and those of people of other faiths, there is an immediate connection. But it is not clear that the pluralist position offers a way of appreciating the persistent differences. In a sense, many of the pluralist constructions still maintain a Christ-centered approach, seeking the sameness on the basis of the central element of one's own faith. The pluralist takes for granted that Jesus Christ has achieved the highest religious goal and offers the opportunity for figures or paths from other traditions to demonstrate that they too have reached this goal. The classic pluralist sees Jesus Christ as moral exemplar and thus allows other traditions to demonstrate also the turn from self-centeredness to God-and-other-centeredness. While helpful in making the connections across different traditions, the pluralist construction does not really allow for the distinctiveness of other faiths. As S. Mark Heim says,

> In [an] indirect but determinative way, Christianity remains normative as a kind of photographic negative. The shape that Christian faith may take is determined by contemporary standards: the specific content inside the silhouette of Christianity may be washed out and replaced with the content of any other faith. But the boundaries of the image remain set and there is no possibility of religions bringing their own profile to change the outline.[33]

Basing so much on sameness, many critics see pluralism as a modified inclusivism, where one tradition is set as the norm against which other religions will be measured. In any case, the emphasis on sameness leaves little room for the exploration and appreciation of differences.

Each of the positions of exclusivism, inclusivism and pluralism shares the characteristic of expecting sameness among all peoples in the world. Exclusivism so clearly expects this sameness that it rejects outright the differences of other religions. Inclusivism uses this sameness as the basis for seeking "Christ" within other traditions; and pluralism similarly seeks sameness, although not explicitly identifying "Christ" as the source of sameness. In these theological responses to religious difference, a self-referential construction of the "other" is employed. Such a construction takes as its starting point a singular norm for all humanity.

As Christian theologies, each identifies Jesus Christ as the norm for all human becoming and all human relatedness to God. From this starting point, all people are judged insofar as they are "just like" Christ, and in turn all religions are judged insofar as they are "just like" Christianity. While the self-referential construction of the other is easily recognized in inclusivist positions such as Rahner's "anonymous Christian" and exclusivist positions that open salvation only to those who explicitly confess Christ, even pluralist positions often rely on a singular norm to be shared among all religions. Thus, implicit in many Christian pluralist positions is a process that affirms Christian relatedness to God through Jesus and seeks to identify a similar relatedness (in moral action or in mystical union) in the forms of other religious traditions. In the theological constructions of exclusivism, inclusivism and pluralism, the "other" is not allowed to be distinctive, but rather is judged by how much "like" the Christian his/her religious practice and achievements are. The exclusivist stance is problematic in its outright rejection of other religions because of their difference. The inclusivist stance of the "anonymous Christian" is problematic in that people of diverse faiths are judged on the basis of Christian characteristics, and thus they are unavoidably seen as deficient in comparison to explicit Christians. The pluralist stance similarly cannot account for the distinctiveness of diverse traditions as positive characteristics. In the pluralist construction, the non-Christian is not an "anonymous" member of the Christian community, but rather, the distinctiveness of any given community is dissolved under the now universalized qualities of singular human fulfillment.

The problem with the self-referential construction of otherness is twofold. First, the Christian judgment of another as "good" insofar as "same" does not let the other be other in his/her own particularity. Religious difference is not a theological resource, but rather, something of a "problem" that Christians must explain away. Second, the description of all religious paths as "same" in some anonymous sense is inadequate to the social scientific data. To discuss the diversity of religions based on self-referential constructions of otherness eliminates both the distinctiveness of Christian witness, practice and aims *and* the distinctiveness of the witnesses, practices and aims of diverse religious communities.

Yet, when one looks at the forms of other religious traditions, there is evidence that the comparison is not between two "like" realities, but rather, that the religions themselves possess radical differences. Looking at the actual practices of religious persons throughout the world, it would seem that people are undertaking a variety of religious pursuits, each form with a particularity that is, perhaps, not comparable to Christ and the specific aims of Christianity. There is a world of stunning variety in the many religious forms.

Anthropologists in Sri Lanka and Southeast Asia, describe a practice in which Buddhist monks are broadcast daily, chanting texts that remind and instruct in the four noble truths, the constituents of grasping, the abodes of being and the eightfold path.[34] Comparativist scholars have a difficult time matching thought for thought the principles of the four noble truths to principles of the Christian tradition. This is especially the case since Buddhism does not use the term "God" as the Christian tradition has understood it. Distinctiveness and difference are evident even in a textbook comparison of Buddhism and Christianity.

When considering differences between Christianity and Hinduism, one might think of the ritual drawings made each day on the floors of Hindu homes to welcome the family's chosen deity,[35] or the more elaborate puja that pays homage to God resident in the temple, with a ritual washing and dressing of the images of the god and goddesses, a food sacrifice, and vedic hymn.[36] Or one might consider the anthropologists' description of the less elaborate but no less sincere offering made to the newly incarnated goddess of AIDS at a roadside stone in rural India,[37] or a gathering outside of

London invoking Agni (God represented in fire) and worshipping the Lord Krishna fully manifest in the sacrificial soma.[38] The distinctiveness of Hinduism challenges the uniqueness of Christ as the bringer of salvation since it understands God manifest and incarnate in innumerable forms.

While Christianity as a tradition is more closely related to Islam than Hinduism, there is no easy way to establish theological harmony between them. Notably, in the pages of the Qur'an, Jesus' status as Son of God is challenged and his divinity is decidedly rejected.[39] For Muslims, it is not Jesus who offers the final affirmation about God, but rather, the text of the Qur'an. This is a difference that radically challenges any anonymous sameness.

When looking at the details of various religious traditions, there does not seem to be a series of similar affirmations about God, world and reality, but rather, there seems to be diversity in the affirmations about God or ultimate reality as expressed in the diverse religious traditions of the world. But the positions of exclusivism, inclusivism and pluralism do not fully account for these differences in their searching for sameness. To varying degrees, these positions embrace the Christian affirmations about the incomprehensible God known in Jesus Christ, but do not sufficiently address the distinctiveness of diverse affirmations about this mystery as they might arise from different religions. Is it not possible that diverse religious forms constitute distinctive awareness of the incomprehensible, overabundant mystery that Christians name "God"? The exclusivist answer is patently, "No." The inclusivist answer tends to see Christ as the measuring stick for any counter-affirmations. And the pluralist shies away from real differences in emphatically making the argument for shared patterns among the religions. These major positions in contemporary thought may affirm Christ's pattern of action, but the engagement with the other does not seem to be able to really listen to and learn from their distinctiveness.

Not only does sameness miss the possibility for learning more about the incomprehensible, overabundant God, it also doesn't seem that conceptual "sameness" has the power to smooth over the lived experience of difference. In concrete encounters with persons of other faiths, the Christian often finds that differences persist and that persons of other faiths seem to be speaking an altogether different language. Instead of the concepts of "God" and "salvation" the Buddhist talks about "Nothingness" and "Nirvana." Instead of the idea that God is revealed uniquely in the human form of Jesus of Nazareth, a Hindu describes the multiplicity of forms through which God incarnates in the world. Instead of a vision of union with the Triune God, Muslims and Jews defend the radical monotheism whereby none is God but God. People of different faiths seem to be describing the world in conflicting and contradictory ways which do not disappear simply because we have *named* the other as the same as ourselves. The diverse descriptions of the world also lead to different patterns of action. These conflicting practices make doctrinal differences apparent in the lived encounter between persons of different religious traditions.

While many discussions of religious pluralism offer only the three positions of exclusivism, inclusivism and pluralism, there is another position that aims to take seriously the particulars of the various traditions. George Lindbeck can serve as representative of this theological "particularism," as he begins from the persistent contradictions in differing views of reality and conflicting patterns of activity in the various religious traditions. Lindbeck reasons that if it seems as if we're speaking different languages when we converse with our neighbors of other faiths, perhaps we are. And it is not only that we're speaking different languages, but these languages and their concepts form our experience of the world and direct us to particular actions. Lindbeck offers a "cultural-linguistic" approach to explain that religious differences persist because religions describe reality in different ways and shape experience distinctively. As Lindbeck explains,

> ...religions are seen as comprehensive interpretive schemes, usually embodied in myths or narratives and heavily ritualized, which structure human experience and understanding of self and world.... Stated more technically, a religion can be viewed as a kind of cultural and/or linguistic medium that shapes the entirety of life and thought.... Like a culture or language, it is a communal phenomenon that shapes the

subjectivities of individuals rather than being primarily a manifestation of those subjectivities. It comprises a vocabulary of discursive and non-discursive symbols together with a distinctive logic or grammar in terms of which this vocabulary can be meaningfully deployed. Lastly, just as a language (or "language game" to use Wittgenstein's phrase) is correlated with a form of life, and just as culture has both cognitive and behavioral dimensions, so it is also in the case of a religious tradition. Its doctrines, cosmic stories or myths, and ethical directives are integrally related to the rituals it practices, the sentiments or experiences it evokes, the actions it recommends and the institutional forms it develops. All this is involved in comparing a religion to a cultural-linguistic system.[40]

In likening religions to cultural-linguistic systems, Lindbeck has in mind the idea that humans need a culture and language in order to navigate the world. Without a language to help organize our thoughts, the stimuli of the universe would be completely overwhelming to us. Language provides the basic tools for identifying elements in the world, while culture offers a way of putting these elements into order. From the use of an object to taste, preference and understanding, culture shapes language into an overarching system that organizes the realities people encounter. In this way of thinking, the only access to "reality" is through the frameworks of culture and tradition in which persons live. As Lindbeck explains, "the cultural-linguistic model is part of an outlook that stresses the degree to which human experience is shaped, molded and in a sense constituted by cultural and linguistic forms."[41] In this perspective, elements of the world and phenomena can be explained in a variety of ways. How one explains them depends, in large part, on the concepts one has to describe and organize the elements at hand. The idea is that the "universe" or "nature" presents uniform but ambiguous stimuli to all persons and that each person is endowed with similar neural apparatus, but neither the stimuli nor the apparatus organize or give meaning to the sense experience itself. The meaning or interpretation of the sense experience comes from the categories and concepts the individual brings to the experience. A group of individuals may all participate in the physical process of eating a meal, but whether each experiences eating beef as harmful to the life of the planet, an abhorrent disgrace of the sacred cow or a barbecued delight depends upon the concepts that are brought to the experience. Similarly, whether the sense experience of the wind in a storm is interpreted as a low pressure system, an act of God or the active spirits of ancestors depends upon the interpretive framework each individual employs. The stimuli presented by the universe is shaped into "data" based on the categories of interpretation the individual uses to organize the sense experience. Exploring this theory of human perception and experience, Lindbeck draws on the work of Thomas S. Kuhn who names the categories of organization "paradigms." Kuhn describes how all persons need a conceptual paradigm through which to organize elements of an otherwise chaotic world when he writes,

> ...something like a paradigm is prerequisite to perception itself. What a man sees depends both upon what he looks at and also upon what his previous visual-conceptual experience has taught him to see. In the absence of such training there can only be, in William James's phrase, "a bloomin' buzzin' confusion."[42]

The stimuli presented by the universe is organized through the forms that a paradigm provides. In the process of organizing stimuli into data, paradigms actually limit what can be known or accessed of reality because they necessarily focus on some details and disregard others as irrelevant.

When Lindbeck applies this social-scientific theory to an understanding of religion, he argues that the texts of a given faith tradition provide the paradigm for the experience of reality for the members of the religious community. The categories of experience made available through the framework of the sacred story uniquely determines what can be experienced and understood of reality. Drawing on empirically oriented theories of religion, Lindbeck adopts the description of each religion as "a distinctive symbolic system linking motivation and action and providing an ultimate legitimation

for basic patterns of thought, feeling, and behavior uniquely characteristic of a given community or society and its members."[43] He
continues, "From the point of view of much, perhaps most, contemporary history, phenomenology, sociology, and psychology of
religion, the faiths by which men live, whether Christian or non-
Christian, are always acquired *ex auditu.*"[44] It is from hearing the
sacred stories that one is given basic categories for encountering
and understanding the mysterious reality of existence. Persons live
in "story-shaped"[45] worlds constructed exclusively from the categories of their scriptures. The sacred stories of one's religion become
the lens through which the world is viewed by religious persons.

The stories of the New Testament and the world described there
are the categorical pattern or paradigm through which Christians
understand and experience the world. The narrative story provides
the language with which to describe human experiences as well as
the concepts and clues for understanding reality. The Christian story
becomes "followable" as it constructs the community's reality and
guides its behavior.[46] Lindbeck encourages Christians to read the
Bible with close attention to its details and the encompassing patterns it offers in order to shape lives and thoughts, modeling them
on the practices visible in the sacred pages. By searching the scriptures and finding clues to how persons have understood the mystery
of existence, Christians are encouraged not only to understand that
mystery in a similar way, but to pattern their lives after the relations evident in the text. In hearing the stories, the hearer is invited
to make them her own, to live the central stories and to become a
character in the unfolding drama of God's relationship to humanity.
By living the pattern of the story in their lives, Christians enflesh the
gospels.

The followable Christian story provides a unifying feature for all
Christians. As Lindbeck describes, "What keeps the church one and
the same through all changes, however great, is that it always re-
members certain specific historical events which culminate in Christ
and continues to hope, not just for any kind of future, but for the
definite future of the Lord's return."[47] The stories and memory of
Jesus Christ are the "objective constant" that persists as the unifying feature of Christian group identity. Just as it has been since

Christianity's inception, so too as far into the future as Christianity exists, "the climactic clues to why we are here and where we are going, the beginning and the end, the Alpha and the Omega, will be found in these tales of life, death, resurrection and the promise of Christ's coming again."[48] Lindbeck radically affirms Christ's pattern as one for Christian action. That is, what makes persons distinctively "Christian" is their being shaped by the story of the New Testament in their relationship to the world and others, and most importantly, in their understanding of God. While many (if not all) theologians would agree that the Christian story ought to shape Christian patterns of action, Lindbeck holds a distinctive understanding of how this story works as he describes it as the singular, comprehensive framework Christians employ for encountering and understanding the world.

This way of thinking about sacred stories allows Lindbeck also to defend the differences found among persons of various faiths. Because the categories of each religion's story are different, that which persons can and do experience is different as well. Differing frameworks of texts, each with a unique narrative, distinctly shape the experience of persons who understand the world through those texts. Lindbeck admits that the focus on particularity within the cultural-linguistic approach and the way frameworks thoroughly shape adherents, "may be useful for the restrictedly ecumenical end of promoting unity within a single religion, but not for the broader purpose of seeking the unity of all religions."[49] Precisely what allows for ecumenical progress (the sharing of a sacred story) makes interreligious relationships more strained. Whereas the New Testament provides all Christians with the same categories for experiencing the universe and organizing its stimuli, the diverse stories of the world's religions provide different categories altogether. If the categories for approaching the same stimuli are different, so too will the organization of data and description of reality be different. Religions are understood as "community-forming semiotic systems" with "uniqueness as formally untranslatable and as materially consisting of the unsubstitutable memories and narratives which shape communal identities."[50] The figures and concepts of sacred narratives are constitutive of the meaning of that narrative and are therefore not interchangeable with the figures or concepts of other stories. The unchanging story of a religious community forms a framework for shaping experience similarly among members of the community. Since the stories of each religion present specific categories in an interconnected web of meaning, seeing the world through them is like approaching the data through different paradigms. In adopting different paradigms, distinct communities know and experience reality in different ways. While a given community is bound together by the same story, the boundaries of the story preclude understanding across difference, because persons are shaped so thoroughly by their particular story. This specificity and particularity of content makes the comprehensive frameworks of the religions incommensurable to one another.

With particular language-constellations derived from their particular life-shaping stories, persons of different traditions are provided with different categories and concepts that shape their experience. With each unique sacred story providing a pattern that is not replicated in other stories, persons of diverse traditions access and experience reality in distinctive ways. The differing frameworks provided by distinct religious traditions produce radically distinct ways of experiencing reality and "fundamentally divergent depth experiences of what it is to be human."[51] Our stories shape us so thoroughly as to create different understandings of the most basic elements of human existence. Further, the cultural linguistic approach

> raises questions regarding the meaningfulness of the notion that there is an inner experience of God common to all human beings and all religions. There can be no experiential core because, so the argument goes, the experiences that religions evoke and mold are as varied as the interpretive schemes they embody. Adherents of different religions do not diversely thematize the same experience; rather they have different experiences.[52]

The logic of this understanding suggests that persons who are shaped by different religious traditions have different experiences of the reality that Christians name "God." This means further, that each tradition shapes its adherents toward different ultimate understandings of the mysterious context of existence and presents them with distinct aims and patterns of action in response to that understanding.

In Lindbeck's approach to religious difference, contemporary Christians can adhere to the traditional affirmations of how Christ's distinctive pattern reveals the mystery of God. Simultaneously, the incomprehensible mystery of God and diverse experiences of God in various traditions are also affirmed. What is missing from his theology is a way for people of differing faith perspectives to converse with and learn from one another. For Lindbeck, a person cannot understand religious statements unless he or she is immersed in that religion's life-world and understands its rules of practice. Because of the incommensurability between frameworks, understanding across distinct frameworks is seen as a possibility only for those who inhabit both frameworks and undertake the long process of acquiring a linguistic competence as a member of both communities. For Lindbeck, this is rare.[53] Categories are not interchangeable and since understanding takes place only within a particular semiotic web, the difficulties of translation and understanding are real. Not only are persons unequipped to compare another's pattern to one's own, the required skills of bilingualism make it nearly impossible to converse across difference. Difference is so radical that there are no tools for making connections.

Just as Rahner is representative of a tendency to seek sameness, there are theologians who align with Lindbeck's emphasis on difference. A more thorough-going application of Lindbeck's cultural-linguistic program can be seen in the work of theologians who defend differences more extensively than Lindbeck himself. The project of S. Mark Heim, for example, pushes the extension of distinctiveness even further, into the eschaton. Drawing out the particularity of religious traditions, Heim insists that there is an integral relationship between the distinctiveness that is experienced on earth and that which is achieved in the eschatological realm beyond this world. For Heim, salvation is not singular, but rather, the diverse forms of religious pursuits achieve diverse forms of salvation. He writes, "The fulfillment we seek need not be everyone's. Ours is not the only salvation: there are others."[54] The vision Heim presents is that the ultimate reality, which Christians name "God," stands in distinctive relationship to persons from diverse faiths. The realm humans "go to" beyond a material existence holds within itself variety of ultimate aims, just as existence in the world sustains a diversity of practices. Heim presents a logical outcome of the argument that our practices, beliefs, stories and actions shape the sorts of lives and aims we achieve. And yet, in emphasizing our differences, Heim seems to suggest that the communities of religions are not only limited in their communicative possibilities here on earth, but are bound in their differences even in the world to come. There are multiple "salvations." Such eschatological divisions would not bode well for the possibilities of cooperation here on earth.

The exploration of Lindbeck's theological program illuminates the ways in which he and other particularists safeguard the distinctions among diverse religious traditions in both their content and aim; however, this particularity is constructed without resources for bridging the distance between persons of different religions. If part of a theology's aim is to provide theological resources for relationships with people of other faiths, a construction of such specific difference and bounded communities provides little with which to create solidarities. In describing the sociological and theological reality of religions, Lindbeck constructs the human family as radically diverse as the result of different frameworks created by our religious stories. He limits the conversation of cooperation within our "divided yet shrinking world."[55] This radical diversity is attended by an incommensurability and the difficulty of understanding across difference. Stories have shaped persons so thoroughly in thought and action that they are different at the very root of who they are. As representative of those positions in the discourse which emphasize difference, Lindbeck's construction illuminates the difficulties of positing radical difference among religions. The problem with these constructions is that they create all too emphatically a separation between Christians and persons of other faiths. And while this is a logical application of cultural-linguistic theory, this separation simply does not match the lived experience of persons in a pluralistic context. That is, people find themselves in connection with others, understanding shared concerns and pursuing shared goals, despite religious differences. Furthermore, in the interconnected world of the twenty-first century, persons cannot afford to forego conversations that would lead to cooperation. The material reality of sharing limited resources and inhabiting the same space means that a theology that cannot envision conversation and cooperation is simply untenable. Persons of different faiths must talk with one another as locations in our world become increasingly pluralistic.

As investigation into the diverse theological responses to religious pluralism can show, contemporary Christian theologians tend to employ strategies of seeking sameness or defending differences. What is notable in placing these two options in close conversation is the recognition that the positions of "sameness" and "difference" both function to distance otherness. In the defense of differences, the idea of incommensurability renders distinct religious traditions as impenetrable to those outside in all but the rarest of cases. And while the search for sameness seems to embrace the other through sameness, the otherness of the other is actually rejected. Difference is not valued as a theological resource but instead it is held at a distance. Neither approach can serve as the foundation for real encounter between persons shaped by distinct religious forms. In one approach, difference is erased and we are encouraged to retreat to the security of sameness. In the other, difference is held at such a distance that the impact of the other can hardly be felt. Where the search for sameness constructs religious identities at the expense of real differences, the defense of difference often compromises the possibility for connections across religions. The contemporary theological discourse on religious pluralism stands at an impasse of sameness or difference.

The root of the impasse can be found in the construction of Christian identity employed in these various theologies. Though the multiple positions of "exclusivism," "inclusivism," "pluralism" and "particularism" present distinct approaches for understanding religious difference in the world, each presents Christian identity as something that is shared among all Christians in distinction to other religions. From among the many ways of being human in the world, the categories "Hindu," "Christian," "Jewish," "Buddhist," "Muslim" or "indigenous/tribal" emerge as identifiable collectivities each of which is defined by a unique set of features shared among the members of the group. The collectivity of persons who share these features make up a given "religion." Religions are seen as communal ways of being in the world marked by certain identifiable characteristics shared among members in distinction to nonmembers.

The arrangement of persons into these categories manufactures "more manageable, transparent populations"[56] as the basis for theological assessment. This process of categorization is defended as a practical necessity: in order to discuss different religions, particularities are subsumed under a limited set of distinctions. But this categorization classifies persons on the basis of a singular identity feature. In order to define Christian identity vis-à-vis other religious identities, one must isolate that feature which will constitute membership in the category "Christian." Logically, there must be a "Christian" element which serves as the defining feature of Christian identity. The subsequent construction of diverse religious communities is based on the same presupposition. The fundamentally defining feature of each community serves to bind persons to those within their religious category and to simultaneously exclude others. The imagined sameness within a community sharpens the differences between the various ways of being in the world, such that theologians can describe "the Muslim perspective" or "Jewish practice."

Having looked at the history of "Christian" encounters with people of other faiths the reader might note from the outset a distinctive problem with the construction of categorical sameness within a "religion." That is, by defining "Christians" as an internally coherent group, this categorization misses the distinctiveness of actual Christians in lived situations. Further, by identifying people on the basis of only one defining feature (e.g., "Christian"), discussions of religious pluralism have erased what is evident in history, namely, that "Christians" are never "Christian" only, but are simultaneously members of a family and participants in a wider community network; they have particular professions, life histories and social locations. This particularity has gone missing in the conversation about "Christians" as a collective. The particularity is even less evident when theologians speak in the collective about "the religions" as distinct entities in contact and conversation with one another.

Despite their best efforts to maintain the lived complexity of religious diversity, theologians rely on conceptual categories that distinguish "the religions" from one another. In doing so, they erase the diversity and complexity of the living persons who are actually engaged in the encounter. Take, for example, John Hick's classic articulation of "the pluralistic hypothesis" where he encourages the reader to see "the religions" as diverse responses to ultimate reality or "the Real." In drawing out the implications of this vision, Hick writes,

> Each tradition will continue in its concrete particularity as its own unique response to the Real. As the sense of rivalry between them diminishes and they participate in inter-faith dialogue they will increasingly affect one another and each is likely to undergo change as a result, both influencing and being influenced by the others. But nevertheless within this growing interaction each will remain basically itself. In this respect, the pluralistic hypothesis makes comparatively little difference to the existing traditions. But in another respect it makes what is for some of them a major difference. For in coming to understand itself as one among several different valid human responses to the Real each will gradually de-emphasize that aspect of its teaching which entails its own unique superiority.[57]

Whether or not we agree with Hick's pluralistic hypothesis and the challenges it holds for religious claims, what is striking is the manner in which Hick hypostatizes "the traditions," construing these conceptual entities as real existents and as subjects in their own right. Not only have the collectives of "the religious traditions" been produced and set alongside one another for comparison, they are now acting as individual subjects: each tradition *participates in dialogue* yet *remains itself, coming to understand itself* in a new way. The traditions themselves take on the characteristics of discrete subjects — dialoguing, reflecting, thinking and acting. Each of the diverse "religions" functions as not only a collectivity, but a collectivity with agency and subjectivity. Such a portrait problematically simplifies complex situations in which living individuals participate in unique dialogues in contexts impacted by material concerns.

In a more recent work, S. Mark Heim argues against the pluralist diminishment of religious particularity, yet he similarly employs "the religions" as collective entities. In this case, the diverse "religions" do not shape persons toward the same ultimate end, but rather they are collectivities through which persons arrive at distinct ultimate aims. Despite the difference between this understanding and Hick's, Heim similarly relies on the collective categorization of "the religions" and constructs his discussion of diverse religious ends by referencing "the Christian account" and "the Buddhist account" of how these ends should be envisaged, as well as collectivizing the traditions in "Buddhist practices" or "Christian expectations."[58] While an alternative vision, Heim still employs conceptual categories of "the religions" as discrete wholes that can be set one against the other for comparison. Again, this renders invisible the actors who create the specific practices through their particular life choices in distinctive, complicated and often messy conditions.

The pattern of thinking in collective then proceeds to consider the problem of how these collectives are related to one another. Following thought patterns like Hick's and Heim's, readers conjure up the image that all "Hindus" or "Muslims" or "Christians" share the same perspectives and understandings with other members of their respective religious communities. Or at least "they" (persons within a given religious community) will share among themselves features they do not share with those of "us" outside that religious community. Setting up "religions" in this way, as homogenous entities with identifiable characteristics shared among persons within their boundaries, the project of comparison takes place on a theoretical level where "the religions" are compared one to another. Here is the heart of the impasse: theologians can theorize a "sameness" among the categories and thus encourage communication across difference on the basis of that sameness; or they can insist on the radical differences between the bounded categories and relinquish the naive hope of understanding across difference. With only one identity feature available for the encounter, the options are either "sameness" or "difference." We have already seen the problems with these options. If all "religions" are essentially the same, we cannot account for, appreciate, or learn from their differences. We miss the possibility for unfolding new affirmations about the over-abundant mystery of God. If, on the other hand, each "religion" is radically different, we lose the common ground necessary for real engagement. Again, we miss the possibility for unfolding new affirmations about God. The realization that neither total sameness nor radical difference works as the basis for real encounter with religious others underscores the failure in contemporary theologies of religious pluralism.

The search for a new way of responding to religious diversity is propelled by the recognition that this diversity permeates the world, and that encounters with difference repeat locally and globally. The interconnected world of globalization renders contact with difference a certainty, through the systems of information, economics and travel that increasingly make our world a single place. At the same time, the power differentials which permeate these systems also mean that space is unequally shared; we are increasingly in need of visions of solidarity that help make shared space truly shared. Christians participate in envisioning a world community through the conversations on religious pluralism and encounters with people of other faiths. But the theologies of the twentieth century have only brought us so far, and have left us at the impasse of sameness or difference. Of course, our theoretical resources have not been exhausted. By employing a new concept of identity we might address the heart of this impasse. Feminist theory offers just such a concept that might provide a framework for interreligious encounters that allow for conversation across difference without erasing particularity and distinctiveness. It is to this new construction of identity that chapter 4 turns.

Chapter Four

WE ARE ALL HYBRIDS

THROUGHOUT HISTORY, Christians have wrestled with the question of how to understand and relate to people of other faiths. This question has become increasingly important in the twenty-first century where the interconnected systems of the globe bring religious difference into contact all the time. One way of considering the issue for today is this: how can Christians recognize and respect the differences of other faiths, while at the same time fostering the connections of solidarity so desperately needed in our "divided yet shrinking world." Asking the question theologically, we might explore how the engagement with religious neighbors not only promotes the healing care practiced by Jesus of Nazareth, but also brings increasing awareness of the mystery of God. As noted in the previous chapter, when twentieth-century theologians explored these issues, they tended to see all religious traditions as basically the same or as radically different. The mode of sameness made difference invisible, while the insistence on radical difference made connections of solidarity all but impossible. What resources are available for a new theology that values differences *and* the connections of solidarity?

To unearth some new resources, one must recognize the problems that restrict the twentieth-century theological options. As described in the last chapter, the heart of these problems lies in the way theologians and thinkers have constructed religious identity as a static feature shared among members of a community in distinction to nonmembers. In this way of thinking about religious identity, religions are viewed in their "specific difference." That is, people of other faiths are first and foremost thought of as different from ourselves by virtue of the religious characteristic that sets them apart. Furthermore, all members of a given religious community who share this characteristic of "specific difference" are visualized as similar to one another and separated from "us" (because we do not share in that one particular characteristic). As one example of specific difference, some thinkers characterize the source of religious identity as connected to the founding figures of each religion. In this way of thinking, then, Christians are distinctive due to their specific difference of following Jesus Christ, just as Buddhists pattern their specific difference on Siddhartha Gautama. Automatically, then, Christians are different from Buddhists who do not follow Jesus Christ, and Buddhists are distinctive from Christians who do not follow Siddhartha. Constructing religious identity on a single feature of specific difference separates human beings by virtue of a single, fundamentally defining feature: a feature rooted in the category of "their religion."

Yet, as Francis Schüssler Fiorenza explains, "such a focus on the specific difference often posits a partial element as the total meaning and so fails to describe adequately a reality's true meaning or identity."[1] Being a Buddhist does not only mean following the path of Siddhartha Gautama; more elements are included as part of this religious identity. Furthermore, all Buddhists do not follow the path of the Buddha in the same way. The variety within the Buddhist community is not accounted for under the construction of "specific difference." The major distinctions of Zen, Mahayana, and Theravada expand into an even greater variety when considering the diversity of geographical, historical and social locations where Buddhists are found. The same is true of Christianity, as Harvey Cox remarks, "In America alone there are estimated to be nearly five hundred separate and distinct forms of Christianity."[2] Add to this the number of Christians in diverse social and geographical contexts around the globe, and we can see that "Christianity" itself is internally diverse. If this diversity within religions exists in sociological data, why has there been a persistence of thinking about religions in the pattern of specific difference that erases this statistical evidence?

The categorization of "the religions" serves as a means to conceptually control an otherwise overwhelmingly complex reality

of religious differences. By constructing religions on their specific difference, theologians and thinkers are able to create more
manageable populations. But this categorization can succeed only
by erasing internal diversity. Feminist theorist Iris Marion Young
would describe this as following a "logic of identity," whereby persons are bound together in their religious identity, and set apart
from those whose religious identity is different. A logic of identity
proceeds by drawing category distinctions to identify what is "in"
or "out" of the totality. Young describes the problems that emerge
as a result:

> Any move to define an identity, a closed totality, always
> depends on excluding some elements, separating the pure
> from the impure. Bringing particular things under a universal
> essence, for example, depends on determining some attribute
> of particulars as accidental, lying outside the essence. Any defi-
> nition or category creates an inside/outside distinction, and the
> logic of identity seeks to keep those borders firmly drawn.[3]

Young's contention is that the logic of identity, while seeking a unity,
dissolves differences as incidental and irrelevant to the sameness
identifiable among members of a group. In the process, the logic
of identity erases specific features of members' identities. Furthermore, the categorization masks an outcome which privileges certain
forms of expression as it eliminates internal diversity. In favor of
collective description, specific difference among the religions eliminates the internal differences of gender, economics, education, race,
geographical and social locations within each religion. Subsum-
ing particularities in proffering collectivity marginalizes and even
erases the expressions of the powerless within the collective. When
Christian theologians argue for a similarity among Christians that
distinguishes them from non-Christians, it is at the expense of the
diversity one might find within Christianity itself. This erasure of
particularity within the collective is the first outcome of employing a logic of identity. A second and simultaneous outcome is
the distancing of otherness. By creating a collective identity to be
shared by those within the category in distinction to those outside

the category, the logic of identity forges intra-religious solidarity through the very process of distancing otherness.

In contemporary theologies of religious pluralism, the various features of one's identity and location are incidental to one's being part of the category "Christian," and so they are ignored. In this construction, one's "Christianness" is an element that can be carved out from the other dimensions of who one is and serve as defining of the collectivity "Christian." The "Christian" aspect of one's identity can be isolated and, dismissing all other features, all who share a "Christian identity" can be grouped together. Bound together with other "like-Christians," persons have little imaginative resources for relating to persons in the bounded categories of other faiths.

But what does it mean to say, "I am Christian"? Theologians like George Lindbeck would claim that this means that a person's understanding of the world has been thoroughly and uniquely shaped by the Christian story.[4] Karl Rahner would see this declaration as providing a countercultural force binding together all who confess it.[5] At the very least, theologians would like to claim that being "Christian" or being grouped within with the religious category of "Christian," means that one's "religious" identity, if not one's entire self-understanding, has been informed by this community alone. Discussing religious pluralism, the category "Christian" becomes visualized as the community of all those who declare "I am a Christian" and this declaration resounds in a global and univocal voice — distinct from the declaration of other religious groupings. Yet, the imaginative echo of a universal declaration of "Christian" identity, ignores the dissonant ways actual Christians understand the claim they are making. If it were the case that all "Christian" identities were formed out of the same religious understanding, there would be greater agreement among Christians themselves. Yet, there exists intra-religious diversity within the "Christian" category. There are differences of interpretation, of aim, of witness and of practice. There are distinctions in the claim "I am a Christian" as it is articulated by a peasant worker and by a multimillion-dollar capitalist. "I am a Christian" means something different to opposing sides in the debate over women's ordination, and has distinct meanings from the perspectives of fundamentalists and feminists. In the course of Christian history, the declaration "I am a Christian" meant something different to different persons in distinct societies, cultures and historical moments. When theologians and thinkers erase these distinctions to present "Christian" identity as different from other religious identities, they separate "Christianness" from other dimensions of each Christian's identity and experience. But is this possible?

Although scholars of religion would group me under the category "Christian" and I myself might identify with that community, it would be difficult to substantiate the claim that my understanding of the world and the shape of my experience within that world is singularly informed by that community. In any given experience of the world or understanding of the world, it is not always possible to identify which feature or features of my identity — Christian, North American, college educated, feminist, married, Midwestern, professorial, familial or otherwise — are informing my interpretation of that experience or understanding. For example, a student comes to me to explain the difficulties of her transition to college, I respond with (what I hope is) an open ear and suggest strategies for coping. Does my response to this student grow out of my Christian understanding? Is it the application of my feminist concerns? Is my response rooted in my experience in a large family with a caring network of support? Or do I mold this encounter by drawing on my pedagogical aims and training in higher education? Perhaps I am responding to this student as I have learned to respond from listening to my husband counsel countless students in high school. As this and an endless list of examples will show, many of the elements of my identity and past experience combine in my one person and inform the response I will formulate. Or as Jean Grimshaw reflects from a feminist perspective, "Experience does not come neatly in segments, such that it is always possible to abstract what in one's experience is due to 'being a woman' from that which is due to 'being married,' 'being middle class' and so forth."[6] What Grimshaw highlights is the natural combination of distinct features into one self. Identity categories are not separable such that one might isolate that slice of identity that informs a given experience.

The dynamic intersection of identity categories helps explain the internal diversity of any given religious tradition. When aspects of identity are forged into a single individual in a way that they cannot easily be compartmentalized, one cannot ask what it means to be a "Christian" without recognizing that the answer is also conditioned by other identity categories. This insight too is provided by feminist theory on the construction of identity. For example, Elizabeth Spelman points out that compartmentalization, although a tempting strategy, does not do justice to the lived experience that our identity features are mutually informing. As Spelman describes it, if identity categories were separable, the multiple factors of our identity would not impact one another and our social location would not matter. She writes, "If my 'womanness' is separable, then I as a woman would still be the same woman I am, even if I happen to have been born into a body of a different color, or even a body of the same color at a different moment in history."[7] If we could truly isolate "Christianness" in the way thinkers do in order to group all "Christians" in a singular category, then I would still be the same Christian I am, even if I happened to have been born in a body of a different color, in a different location or in another cultural context. But if I had been born today into the body of a female among the Christian minority in Korea, my experience of "being a Christian" would, I suspect, be different. My claim of Christian identity might stand in solidarity with the identities of my fellow women struggling for human wholeness in a patriarchal context and might also stand in solidarity with women and men resisting neo-colonialist practices and the dehumanization of poverty. These men and women with whom I might share my cultural or ideological identity, may or may not be Christian, since the population of Christians in Asia numbers only about 5 percent. In this context, I might understand my Christian identity to be one among many resources for envisioning the wholeness of my cultural community. Like Chung Hyun Kyung, I might revision Christ as a shamanic healer at the intersection of Christian and indigenous religious forms, identifying Christ in precisely this way so as to offer a remedy for the healing of brokenness in a postcolonial Asia struggling against poverty, imperialism and sexism.[8] My Christian identity and my understanding of Christ would be shaped by the other dimensions of my social condition.

The particularity of each Christian creates the internal diversity within the collective. Using the resources of feminist theory, we can challenge the logic of identity and rethink "specific difference" to recognize that the categories of all religions are made up of diverse identities. Each of these identities is constructed out of the intersection of multiple fundamentally defining features — religion, race, class, gender, nationality, ethnicity, profession, sexual orientation, and so forth. Our religious identities are not sui generis and unaffected by other dimensions of who we are; rather, our very understanding of the religious dimension of our identity is informed by the diverse features of our location and experience. There is no "Christian" identity, only Christian identities impacted by race, gender, class, ethnicity, profession, and so on. In contrast to the way thinkers have tended to consider religious persons as identifiable through a singular feature ("Christianness" or "Buddhist identity") and have subordinated all other aspects of identity to this religious dimension, feminist thought emerging from women's experience suggests that each individual has multiple and mutually informing aspects of identity. One's religious identity is not isolatable as "Christian" only, but one's "Christianness" and the experience of "being Christian" is informed by a myriad of fundamentally defining features. Thus, each of us is formed by a web of identity. As Morwenna Griffiths describes, the self is "intricate, entangled and interlaced, with each part connected to other parts."[9] As intricate, each self is not the solid entity of a single identity, but rather is forged at the intersection of a multiplicity of fundamentally defining features. Such multiplicity cannot be dissected such that each feature remains pure and untouched by the others, but as mutually informing they are "entangled and interlaced." One's sexual orientation, gender, age and economic status indeed inform one's very Christian identity. Seeing each individual identity as web, we can no longer afford a simple designation of "Christian," "Muslim" or "Jew," instead, the category itself is made up of a collective diversity wherein each individual is a *particular* Christian, a particular Muslim or a particular Hindu, with identity features irreducible to the collective.

The recognition that Christian identity is always impacted by other features of our identities helps us read the diversity in Christian history in a new way. In each of the episodes recounted in chapter 2, the reader has seen that individual Christian responses to persons of other faiths depended in part on the other features of identity which impacted the individual in context. The "Christian" identity of the earliest Christians was often informed also by their Jewish identity or Greek identity. They were simultaneously family members and socially related to their respective Jewish or Greek communities. The responses to religious difference they formed were impacted by the diversity of sites on which they overlapped with their neighbors of other faiths. The "Christian" identity of Matteo Ricci and Roberto de Nobili was impacted by their adoption of the lifestyle of native peoples in China and India; thus Ricci saw the resonance with Confucian forms, and de Nobili heard the perspective of his Hindu companions. The identity of their "profession" or "chosen lifestyle" as ascetics and scholars informed their understanding of their Christian identity as it overlapped with their companions of other faiths. The "Christian" identity of Bartolomé de Las Casas was impacted by his experience with the native peoples of Latin America. He recognized how they shared with him their complex humanity as rational, emotional, political and artistic beings. This shaped his positive response to the indigenous peoples but also his negative response to his Christian compatriots who denied the very humanity of native peoples. The intersecting dimensions of identity and experience shaped each of these Christian responses in history.

In history and today, Christian identities are always "hybrid," that is, they are created by intersecting with other categories of identity. In any group of Christians — from local congregations to a global community — the collective will reflect a diversity. The category "Christian" itself is not homogenous. The hybrid identity of each member produces a religious community of infinite internal diversity. Theorists might say that the category "Christian" is not a solid totality but a category made up of multiplicity and fragmentation. Griffiths describes the result of such a recognition when she writes,

The acceptance of fragmentation is the relinquishing of an inappropriate dream of purity, as well as a relinquishing of the wish for the unity of the subject.... Indeed, the problem of fragmentation takes on an entirely new look when it is recognized that most people will not identify 100 percent with any group in which they find themselves. We are all hybrids. A group need not strive after purity. To do so is to force its members into making a more than 100 percent identification, a condition in which much of their experience and interests are stifled.[10]

If the experience of being "Christian" is also informed by other dimensions of identity, then no one will identify 100 percent with the categorical grouping of "Christianity." Some dimensions of identity will affiliate also with the category "gender" or the category of "profession" or the category of "generation." The understanding of what it means to be "Christian" is informed by these other dimensions of an individual's identity. While this means that the collective of Christians will be fragmented and that there will not be 100 percent identification among all members of the group, this doesn't need to be a negative reality. In fact, the diversity within any given community allows for hybrid identities that can foster connections outside that particular grouping. This is possible because each strand of the web of identity has been formed relationally through engagement in other communities. Although shaped, in part, by affiliation with a religious community, individual identities have also been fostered in conversation with other communities — the community of family, profession, generation, nationality, gender and so forth. While not identifying completely with any one given category/community, each individual partially identifies with many. The idea of incomplete identification *within* a category can be embraced as the potential for Christians to forge solidarities *outside* the Christian community. As Martha Minnow suggests, "No one identity category, sexual orientation, gender, ethnicity, class, family status captures [an individual's] whole world. These very differences afford chances for connection.... "[11] If every member does not identify 100 percent with the categorical group of "Christian," then a

certain percentage of *each* member identifies with a different categorical grouping or groupings. The Christian, then, is at home in
community with other Christians, but the multiple facets of his/her
identity allow him or her to forge innumerable solidarities by virtue
of association in multiple communities. It is our internal diversity as
a Christian community that affords an infinite number of possible
sites for forging solidarities beyond our given religious category.

How does the foregoing discussion of identity as hybrid relate
to the challenges of religious diversity explored in the preceding
chapters? One of the criteria set out for a new theology of religious pluralism was that it allow for deep engagement with people
of other faiths. Such engagement might draw on similarities but
must also address directly the differences. Thinking about our religious identities as socially constructed and formed in conversation
with multiple communities is a new resource for enacting solidarity
across religious differences. Just a few examples of how this can
occur may help to explain why envisioning categories of internal
diversity is an important shift in our thinking about religious pluralism. In the past, religious categories have been created on the basis
of a single criterion. This makes only one identity feature available
for making a connection with others. One might assume a shared
connection with others within one's religious community, but find
it difficult to envision the relationship between the singular "Christian" identity and the religious identity of the neighbor. This is the
way theologians of the recent past have considered the question,
leading to the impasse of sameness or difference. Whereas constructing religious categories on a singular criterion makes available
only one identity feature on which to make a connection (assessing
the other's religious identity on the basis of either "sameness" or
"difference"), constructing religions as communities of internal diversity allows for the partial identification of overlapping identities
where a variety of identity features hold the potential for making
connections.

In the field of religious studies and interreligious theology, this
process of partial identification has fostered collaborative efforts
across the boundaries of religious traditions. This is seen in some
texts of feminist theology including *Womanspirit Rising*,[12] *Weaving*

the Visions,[13] and *After Patriarchy: Feminist Transformations of the World Religions.*[14] In these writings, feminists from across a variety of traditions come together to address shared concerns and religious insights. These collaborations did not begin from an assumed sameness among the diverse religions, nor did they insist on the incommensurable differences between them. Rather, drawing on the multiple aspects of their identities, religious feminists collaborated precisely on a hybrid religious identity — each was simultaneously a member of a "religious tradition" and a "feminist." In these collaborative texts of feminist theology, thinkers identified patterns in feminist spirituality that transgressed the boundaries of religious traditions. The creative exchange of methodologies and the shared struggle for gender equality encouraged solidarity among feminists, despite being affiliated with distinct religious communities. In these projects, religious differences were not dissolved, nor were persons distanced as the result of particularity, but rather, solidarity was forged in particularity. The association with other feminists of diverse traditions informed each individual's own understanding of the religious community in which she was based. As Carol Christ recalls,

> I vividly remember the days when the women and religion section [of the American Academy of Religion] was a place where feminists in religion engaged in dialogue across religious boundaries. I believed that we were working together to transform and recreate religious traditions.[15]

In these projects and others, we can see the potential for solidarity by virtue of the multiplicity in our religious identities.

To extend the example of solidarity across differences, we might envision other acts of resistance to social injustice in lived collaborations. For example, a group from a Christian church may live out their commitment to Jesus' life practice by participating in the struggles of immigrant families new to the area. Their strength in doing so arises from their internal multiplicity as they provide legal referrals, companionship, health care information and conversation partners for language practice. The "feminist-Christian" who participates in the effort does so to live out her feminist *and* Christian concerns. Yet, she may find that a Muslim friend wishes to join the effort from out of his own commitment to social justice, and a Buddhist neighbor out of empathy for the plight of the refugee. The participation of Muslim friends and Buddhist neighbors in this project may, in turn, open up the opportunity for involvement to a wider segment of their respective religious communities. Overlapping concerns can spread wider the net of solidarity. Yet, while working alongside persons of other faiths, the distinctiveness of their religious perspective is not erased, and communication does not take place on some newly found sameness within the two religions. Rather, as members of multiple communities simultaneously, each possess a multilingualism through which a shared language can be found. In the process of conversations about the struggles of the marginalized (or even discussions about work or neighborhood concerns), ideas specific to another's religious tradition might arise. Here we might envision what Rita Gross describes as the "comparative mirror," an epistemological tool that enables us to see practical and religious "alternatives that we would be unlikely to imagine on our own."[16] Collaborative efforts can bring to the surface the unique resources of particular traditions. Thus, in forming the net of solidarity, it is not only elements of overlapping identity that are valued (for providing sites of connection) but elements of difference which offer new ways of understanding the common task.

This way of viewing identity allows for encounter and what might be called "communicative exchange." By embracing identity as multifaceted, commonalities can be identified that sustain conversation and solidarity without reducing the complexity of differences that persist. Importantly, difference also can be valued as a resource in the exchange. Through sharing diverse perspectives, persons learn more about what it means to be human. Conversation partners are offered new ways of understanding existence in the universe. Thinking theologically, this encounter and exchange in overlapping identity allows for new awareness of the mystery of God.

But in the encounter of living, breathing, embodied persons, who bring to the exchange all of who they are, the sites of sameness and difference cannot be predetermined. The connections will be made on any number of unexpected and often random features of identity. They will arise from the fact that each is not Muslim and Christian only (for example) — but a particular Muslim, of a particular age, from a particular background and family, meets a particular Christian whose background and experience have some hidden elements of overlap. The lifetime of being a Christian and having particular experiences has shaped the "Christian" just as the lifetime of being a particular Muslim has shaped the "Muslim." The backgrounds and experiences, thoughts and hopes serendipitously meet at particular moments over questions and conversation distinctive to a given encounter. If the Christian were to encounter another Muslim whose background and experience was different, he or she could not expect to discover the same sites of connection found previously, even with another Muslim. But in each meeting, some sites of connection can be expected, even if they cannot be identified in advance. The many features of each person's identity that are brought to the encounter means that if space is given to truly encounter the other, it is hard to imagine that some points of contact would not be found. This point is important because it underscores the exponential diversity within each tradition, and the practically infinite insights to be gained through communicative exchange.

We come to the encounter — to each encounter — unable to say where we will find sameness and difference. We recognize our inability to understand or control the differences we might find. As Iain Chambers explains,

> To hold on to the uncertainties of this mutual interrogation is imperative. Otherwise my desire continues to reproduce the cycles of hegemony that subject the other to *my* categories, to *my* need for alterity. Then my recognition of difference merely becomes the prison for the object of my desire. Requested to carry the burden of "authenticity," of "difference," of "post-coloniality," the other continues to be exploited, to be colonised, in another name.[17]

We do not come to the encounter knowing *a priori* what will be the result. Openness to the unanticipateable multiplicity inherent in each person allows the encounter to take place in freedom. It also respects the autonomy of those we encounter. Allowing the other to be other means that we cannot say in advance what "Christian thought" says about him or her. Instead, we remain open to the newness of each meeting, relinquishing the possibility of a controlling knowledge. Practitioners of interreligious dialogue on a more formal level describe this phenomenon of being unable to anticipate the outcome of each conversation. The encounter with the "other" is neither one of total sameness nor unbridgeable difference, but the encounter and exchange is quite unpredictable. The preconceptions of what "Buddhist thought" or "Christian doctrine" means are shattered by actual conversations between particular Buddhists and particular Christians whose own understanding and interpretations of the thought and doctrine of their tradition varies widely. As a creative exchange, one never knows quite where the conversation will lead as conversation partners dance between sameness and difference, at times seeing clearly and recognizing conceptual agreement, at other times speaking past one another and not fully understanding the other's perspective.

In the ongoing process of conversation and learning from the perspective of others, identity is seen not only as multifaceted but, in fact, as dynamic. As feminist theorist Ann Ferguson describes, we might think of the self as "an existential process." By this she means that the person who stands face-to-face with the "other" in an encounter is not a static, unified individual, formed once and for all prior to the encounter. Rather, the various aspects of the self, by being nurtured in distinctive communities and activated in actual exchanges, grow and develop throughout the entirety of one's life. As various aspects of the self are developed in diverse social settings, one's overall sense of self changes at different times and in different contexts.[18] As an existential process, the self and one's identity are not an unchanging core defined by the features of one's gender, religion or race; rather the self is dynamic and continually in process. Identities are always changing and constantly reinvented in a complex nexus of personal and political, material and social, economic and spiritual factors. Thinking of the self and our religious identities as a continual process also affords new possibilities for openness in contact with religious difference. Understanding the

self as an existential process we might see that individuals are required "chronically to construct their identities in social interaction,
rather than to find them in stable social roles and associated subject positions."[19] This means that our sense of self and identity
is continually reconstructed in the multiplicity of our interactions.
Identity — even religious identity — is not given once and for all
with a collective label of our "religion." Rather, the process of
identity development takes place throughout one's life. Conceptualizing identity as a *verb*, the negotiation of religious identity is a
lifelong activity that occurs through historical, contingent, complex
and multiple processes.[20] From a feminist perspective, identity is not
something we inherit or are born into; it is not pregiven with the an-
alytical or religious categories identified in our discourses. Rather,
identity and the emergence of the self occurs relationally. "Self" is
contingent and negotiated; "Identity [is] constructed, reconstructed
and negotiated in relationships of love, resistance, acceptance and
rejection."[21] Furthermore, the relational construction of identity is
not vis-à-vis a generalized other which one can define and control.
As psychoanalytic feminist Nancy Chodrow argues, in human development, "adequate separation, or differentiation, involve[s] not
merely perceiving the separateness, or otherness of the other. It in-
volves perceiving the person's subjectivity and selfhood as well."[22]
Thus, identities are formed in relation to living persons who are recognized as selves. In today's context of globalization, the embodied
persons with whom we engage and in whose presence we ongoingly
construct our identities are often persons of different religious traditions. Identity — even Christian identity — is formed in contact
and conversation with religious others.

But the process of developing Christian identity in contact and
conversation with religious difference is not at all new. The reality of overlapping, hybrid and dynamic identities can be seen in
the history of Christian encounter from the beginning. In antiquity, Christian identities emerged in conversation with the religious
traditions of Judaism, Greece and Rome; and possibly even Buddhism and Hinduism. Embedded in social networks, these meetings
out of which Christian identity emerged were not "religious" only,
but were intersected with social, economic, and political concerns.

The distinctiveness of Christian identity did not erase the features of identity as members of families and tradesmen or members of larger social and political contexts. When we recognize that Christians in the early church were not Christian only, but often simultaneously Jewish or tradespeople and certainly members of wider family and social networks, we begin to get the sense of the "others" whose perspectives helped shape Christian identity. In the controversy over Christian participation in the synagogue, we might envision fellow Jews questioning the legitimacy of this new way of understanding Jewish identity. In the case of the Christians at Corinth, lying beyond Paul's letter we can faintly hear the invitations to meals at communal dining areas of pagan temples extended by non-Christian friends or family members at times of festival in this cosmopolitan city. We might even imagine their puzzlement over invitations rejected or second-guessed. The visitors to Alexandria might have had conversations with traders that would have somehow revealed the alternative religious beliefs being systematically formulated and reflected upon by religious leaders and wider Christians as well; and when Christian tradespeople traveled the Roman trade routes, encountering the other in his or her home country might require delicate concern for social/religious practices as good business practices. Thinking from the perspective of the others of Roman authority, Christians appeared to be a countercultural sect that threatened the social fabric of the empire. Each of these examples reveals that "Christian" identity has been shaped in response to the lived encounter with religious others. Identity has never been a static, given reality, but dynamically forged in contact and conversation.

This dynamism of identity and the characteristic fostering of religious understanding in conversation with others have had the outcome of weaving religious identities across the categories of "the religions." This was certainly the case as the earliest Christians developed their identities in contact and conversation with Judaism. The distinction of Jewish and Christian was not at all universal in the early centuries, and the family resemblance between them persists. Rather than two vastly different categories, Judaism and Christianity meet at points of contact and overlap. In the ancient world this was true also of Christianity and Greek traditions, where Christians drew on Greek thought as a resource and formed an overlap between categories. In more modern contexts, this weaving of differences has taken place across many other religious communities. In many missionary contexts, hybrid religious identities were formed that embraced multiple religious traditions simultaneously. Thus, while newly converted Christians participated in the faith life of this community, they may also have called on their religion of origin for additional resources. For example, African Christians in the nineteenth century had recourse not only to Jesus and the saints as mediators of God, but called upon their local ancestors as well. For Africans who developed their religious identities in Cuba, the emergent form of Santeria came to be practiced in combination with Roman Catholicism. In many cases, indigenous practices merged with newly presented Christian forms to create a single religious system. For example, the traditional healing practices of African Traditional Religion, in which humans were the conduit of divine power, could be integrated into Christian rituals themselves.[23] The practices of syncretism can be seen among the populations of slaves who were "converted" to Christianity and "conformed" to the religion of the master under conditions of unparalleled restraint. Despite the possible consequences that might result from the hand of a slave owner, African slaves continued to practice indigenous forms of religiosity as they were exported to the so-called New World.[24] These examples suggest "conversion" to Christianity has included a synthesis of religious traditions that challenges the distance and the borders between Christian and non-Christian religious forms. Similar evidence of religious blending can be seen in almost every missionary site around the world.

The construction of hybrid religious identities is not only evidenced in the complex encounter of colonial spaces, but continues as a reality in the lives of many Christians throughout the globe today. In Peru and Bolivia, Catholic Christianity and Aymaran religion intersect in the lives of many Christians; in South Asian countries Buddhism and Christianity meet. Chile is a context that reflects "a syncretism that brings together elements from traditional Catholicism, and indigenous religions, Eastern religions, current science and technology and new age practices."[25] In India, Catholic saints can be seen incorporated into the Hindu villagers' pantheon of gods and goddesses.[26] Chinese Christians often recognize Confucian elements in their practice of Christianity, and Vietnamese-American Catholics might maintain Buddhist shrines in their homes. A Christian in Nigeria may turn in times of crisis to African Traditional Religion. Looking at the Christian community through the lens of hybridity, we can also recognize theologians shaped by multiple traditions, as in the case of Raimon Panikkar who is informed by Hinduism and Christianity.[27] In many places within our global community today, the hybrid stands as a figure of double consciousness, sharing identity features with multiple religious communities.

If one thinks with the concept of predetermined Christian identity, the hybridity of syncretism is seen as compromising Christian identity. But considering syncretism from the perspective of those who practice it would suggest a more positive assessment. Persons have recognized the truth of Christianity but have insisted also on the truth and life-giving possibilities of their native tradition. They have appreciated the resources of multiple religious forms. In their lives these global Christians have embraced both Christianity and other religions as life-giving patterns of orientation. Persons who locate themselves in multiple religious communities at the same time ignore the boundaries that have been constructed between the communities. They thus create a pattern that others might follow. As Homi Bhabha expresses it, the hybrid "breaks down the symmetry and duality of self/other, inside/outside."[28] With hybrid religious identities forged at the passage between categories, we are encouraged to see the boundaries of categorization as permeable, rather than clearly delimited.[29] Hybrid religious identity challenges the "fact" of religious pluralism whereby our religious identities first and foremost divide us from one another. One's "Christian" identity ought not be thought of as isolated from other communities, nor as unaffected by so-called "non-Christian" communities (religious or cultural). The categories themselves can be envisioned as unbounded and permeable, where identities are forged in the shifting between.

Locating the dual spaces of feminist and post-colonial theory, Trinh T. Minh-ha articulates the multiple locations of shifting identity, illuminating both the ways in which each individual occupies multiple locations and how those categories we use to distinguish differences are inadequate to the play of sameness and difference that characterizes all relationships. She writes,

> "I" is, therefore, not a unified subject, a fixed identity, or that solid mass covered with layers of superficialities one has gradually to peel off before one can see its true face. "I" is, itself, infinite layers. Its complexity can hardly be conveyed through such typographic conventions as I, i, or I/i. Thus I/i am compelled by the will to say/unsay, to resort to the entire gamut of personal pronouns to stay near this fleeing *and* static essence of Not-I. Whether I accept it or not, the natures of *I, i, you, s/he, We, we, they*, and *wo/man* constantly overlap. They all display a necessary ambivalence, for the line dividing *I* and *Not-I, us* and *them*, or *him* and *her* is not (cannot) always (be) as clear as we would like it to be. Despite our desperate, eternal attempt to separate, contain, and mend, categories always leak.[30]

As a dynamic and shifting identity, constantly reinvented in new contexts and under diverse conditions, the "self" (Trinh's "I") cannot be defined once for all, but takes up a variety of aspects. The constantly shifting dynamic identity of the "other" similarly takes in a variety. Thus, the natures of "self" and "other" shift, transform and overlap so that the dividing lines between self and other are not always clear. Trinh announces that categories always leak across the dualisms of male/female, I/not-I, we/they; and, we might see now, the unstable categories of Christian/non-Christian. We are all hybrid. The categories do not contain all of who we are, and the dynamic elements that layer ourselves are constantly shifting, overlapping even with persons of another faith. This breaks down the duality between self and other, breaking open the conceptual space to reimagine bonds of solidarity

As we get to know people of other faiths, perhaps even the categories that separate us in the "fact" of religious pluralism can

be challenged. As Francis Clooney writes, "If an increasing expertise in the details of traditions, coupled with the loss of an
all-encompassing vocabulary by which to explain the data, demands
that we question the presumption of neatly separate religions separated across divides that need to be bridged, then we find ourselves
in a situation that is too complex for immediate systematization,
particularly when the language of systematization is inevitably laden
with older and no longer entirely adequate reifications of religions
as separate entities."[31] The lines of communication that are opened
by sharing lives in proximity to one another can lead to communicative exchange and increased understanding of other faiths. As
we foster these relationships and increase our understanding, the insights and information we gain from witnessing the power of other
religious traditions might not fit neatly in the categories of "religions" that divide us from one another. In recognizing our own
multiple selves and shifting identities, we are given the freedom to
reinvent religious identities that create solidarity. Far from a core
and unchanging "Christian" identity, even Christian identity is one
which can be informed by contact with different religious forms.

The recognition of multifaceted identities that arises from feminist thought provides the framework for a theology of religious
difference where encounter is encouraged and communicative exchange possible. This construction envisions a solidarity concerned
with the material conditions of our world. But this insight into identity must be joined with a systematic theology in order to develop
in continuity with the tradition of Christian thought. It is to this
systematic theology that chapter 5 turns.

Chapter Five

LIVING
RELIGIOUS PLURALISM

IN A WORLD where religion fuels global conflicts and allegiances
to faith communities can create local divisions, the need for
understanding across difference is essential. As globalization rapidly
transformed the twentieth century, theologians attempted to address
this pressing need by offering responses to religious difference consistent with Christian belief. These theologies of religious pluralism,
however, failed in their ability to provide explanations of religious
diversity that appreciated the distinctiveness of particular communities. When they did defend differences, it was at the expense of
envisioning strategies for engagement across difference. At the close
of the twentieth century, Christian theology viewed religious difference as a problem to be overcome. At the opening of the twenty-first
century, perhaps there is room to see the differences of the religious
traditions of the world as gifts bestowed on the human community.
The theology of this chapter attempts this task and envisions the
reality of living religious pluralism.

This theology begins and ends in incomprehensibility — in the
mystery surrounding all of existence. As humans, we come into this
world contingent and not in control, and ultimately realize that
all that is arises from a complex and mysterious origin. This mystery, from which we come and to which we ultimately return, is
what Christians name "God." In the words of Gordon Kaufman,
"God...is to be understood as the underlying reality (whatever
it may be) — the ultimate mystery — expressing itself throughout
the universe and thus also in this evolutionary-historical trajectory

which produced humanity."[1] But this mystery is encountered not only at the origin and end of existence. The experience of the world itself is saturated with the awesome and the inexplicable. God is the mystery in which we live and move and have our being.

The ultimate context of existence is incomprehensible mystery. It is mystery that sustains and surrounds us from birth until death. Humans encounter this mystery in contemplating the questions at the edge of our existence — from where did we come? Ultimately, where are we going? But it is not only in moments of profound reflection — standing at the ocean's edge, gazing at the stars or meditating in silence — that we sense this mystery. Each day as we strive to organize the data of our existence, we can recognize mystery in the complex world we inhabit. We live in a universe that we strive to understand, but which, in its totality, is beyond our grasp. The universe is overwhelmingly complex in its reality and diversity. And just as humans grasp realities through explanation, new realities are discovered. This novelty and the complexity of existence hints toward a boundless source of being that is the mysterious reality of God. God's overabundance coursing through creation communicates to us far more than the human mind could understand. This renders the world an overwhelmingly complex arena for the process of human life. Bombarded by the overabundance of creation, face-to-face with the mystery of existence at every turn, the human person requires some orientation to an otherwise overwhelming reality. Here arise the stories that sustain us.

Throughout history, humans have tried to understand this universe and our place in it. We have created connections and found explanations for our experiences. From the originary myths of peoples around the globe to the techniques of scientific explanation, each seeks to organize and explain the existence we inhabit, the mystery in which we have our being. The numerous branches of science (physical, chemical, molecular, sub-atomic) as well as the vast studies of humanity (in philosophy, anthropology, psychology, art, literature, history and religion), all represent the human attempt to reflect upon and explain our experience. Yet, we recognize that none of these explanations can provide all the answers. Each discipline speaks to particular aspects of our existence and, by necessity, ignores other aspects. As they organize the data of the universe, each framework presents a meaningful explanation and orientation; but we can recognize that each does so in a distinctive way. Thus, we see a wide variety of ways to provide explanation and orientation in our complex existence. Furthermore, anomalies and newness constantly challenge comprehensive frameworks, necessitating changes in our explanations as we consider new information or discover new realities. The ongoing creation of new paradigms is a response to the novelty that arises in the world.

How do we make sense of the great variety of ways people understand and experience the "reality" of our shared existence? Here we might follow George Lindbeck's cultural-linguistic model to understand persons as shaped by the significant stories of their culture and tradition. Lindbeck sees the pattern of cultural-linguistic meaning embedded in the classic texts of a given culture. These texts serve both to reflect the ethos of a given people and shape future generations. Lindbeck suggests that, "Texts project worlds in which entire cultures can and have lived."[2] The familiar and honored classics of a culture influence the way people understand their lives because these classics present imaginative worlds which mirror and mold the world persons encounter day to day. In reading the classic texts of another culture, one might miss the complexity of meaning and the nuance of actions; but in reading the classic texts of one's own culture, one experiences them as providing a thick description of life and "the way things are." By suggesting that classic texts provide categories for experience and thought-patterns for the group, Lindbeck underscores also that experiences are particular to localized communities. Shaped by the formative patterns embedded in their classic texts, persons of a particular culture understand and experience the world in ways different from persons of another culture. In the diverse cultures and their accompanying languages, different interpretive frameworks provide the vocabulary and logic with which individuals experience and understand the world, reality and the ultimate mystery of existence. These frameworks are constituted by the philosophies, knowledges and classic stories of each culture, so that the categories of experience made available through each framework uniquely determine what can be experienced and understood. Because the categories available are different, that which persons of various cultural frameworks can and do experience is different as well. Different frameworks organize the sensory data of reality differently and, in turn, access reality in distinct ways. The diversity of schemes or paradigms for experiencing reality produce a pluralism in humanity's actual experience of reality.

The existence of different paradigms for organizing reality can have benefits and drawbacks. On the negative side, conflicts we experience locally and globally often seem to arise from different descriptions of "the way things are" and "the way things ought to be." These conflicts are often deeply rooted because they are founded on the understanding of reality structured by a given cultural community. In the many heated disputes of our world today, different descriptions of reality for competing parties make conflicts irresolvable. In the long-standing conflicts over territories, the "homeland" often belongs by right to both parties as this right is outlined in their cultural histories. In the debate on abortion rights, both sides may agree that the murder of human persons is wrong, but each has organized the data and definition of the fetus in different ways so that their positions ultimately conflict. And the list could go on. The diverse paradigms for organizing the data of reality lead to competing and conflicting descriptions of "reality" and the appropriate actions in response.

While the diversity of cultural-linguistic frameworks indeed poses problems in terms of the conflicting accounts of reality they engender, this same diversity holds potential for positive possibilities. For example, at times, a given paradigm is limited in its explanatory power and can be augmented or replaced by alternative ways of viewing the same reality. The growing trend toward holistic medicine in the United States is a prime example of new possibilities opened up only because of existing differences in cultural-linguistic understandings of human well-being. Where Western medicine has been founded on the treatment of bodily ailments and disease as physical conditions, the long standing traditions of Eastern medicine look to the mental and spiritual dimensions of the patient for clues. These traditions have been seen as competing patterns for understanding wellness, and in the United States, the alternative of Eastern forms often has been looked down upon as an inferior form of medicine. Yet, increasingly, the medical profession in the United States is exploring and employing strategies of mind and body that grow out of the competing paradigm of the East. Only with the tradition of different ways of approaching reality can alternative possibilities emerge.

The idea of competing paradigms might also explain the diversity of religions, if we understand the text of the community to shape their respective understandings of the world. As Lindbeck argues, believers see the world imaginatively through "scriptural lenses" allowing the structure of the sacred narrative to organize the sensory stimuli of the world and shape experiences of the world. In this cultural-linguistic understanding, religious communities are "story-shaped"[3] and their "canons function to help construct communities"[4] by similarly shaping experiences. In the sacred classics, we find the symbolic language that tries to offer ultimate answers to the fundamental questions of existence, pointing especially to a transcendent reality that is beyond the reach of science and human knowledge. The stories of our religions orient us to this transcendent dimension — the ultimate mystery of existence. Persons engaged in religious communities may find significant answers and subtle clues to existence in the lines of their sacred scripture. Yet, while Christians may find orientation to the world through the story of "God," "Christ" and "salvation," people of other faiths describe the world in different terms. Instead of the concepts of "God" and "salvation" a Buddhist may talk about "Nothingness" and "Nirvana." Instead of the idea that God is revealed uniquely in the human form of Jesus of Nazareth, a Hindu describes the multiplicity of forms through which God incarnates in the world. Instead of salvation in union with the Triune God, Muslims and Jews defend the radical monotheism whereby none is God but God. The world and its mystery are being described in conflicting ways. And as the world is described in contradictory ways, distinct realities provide sites for orientation and diverse patterns of action proceed in response.

But Lindbeck's cultural-linguistic theory of religious difference needs to be modified in order to match the data of history and to provide a way for communicating across cultural-linguistic differences. Specifically, Lindbeck argues that individuals are comprehensively shaped by the story of their sacred scripture and that all those shaped by the same story will experience the world and pattern their actions in a similar way. Yet, his construction of religious shaping seems inaccurate to the lived experience of intra-Christian difference in history. The empirical data shows that the Christian story has shaped Christians in history in a wide variety of ways, reflected in the internal diversity in the category of "Christians." The reason that Lindbeck's theory fails at this point is that he is working with a concept of Christian identity as static and rooted in an unchanging, singular Christian story. As such, Lindbeck's theory has limited explanatory power in discussing the wide variety found among actual Christians. A change in the concept of "identity" can modify Lindbeck's theory to match the data of history and provide a resource for the future. Instead of the static, singular story that shapes all Christians, consider the feminist construction of identity as multifaceted and the Christian story as one among many that shapes actual Christians.

Embracing the idea that multiple stories shape people, the cultural-linguistic framework expands to include the intertextuality of stories woven together to provide distinctive and dynamic ways of understanding existence. People are shaped not only by the story of their religion, but also by the stories that adhere to culture, nation or ethnicity. People are shaped by the stories told that form gender and racial identity. Each of these stories is also impacted by science, economics, philosophy, and the story of history. Because each member of a religious community is not "religious" only, he or she has learned the stories of these other communities. The stories intersect so that the understanding of the sacred story is impacted by a multiplicity of factors including race, gender, culture, social location, economic status, age, ethnicity, national identity, social position and so forth. Intersectional membership in more than one group alters one's horizon for understanding the community's central story.[5] Yet, just as the story of science, for example, informs a person's reading of scripture, the intertextual process of weaving stories together should mean that the story of scripture also guides the reading of science.

Intersectional membership and contact sets up the conditions for communicative exchange across different communities.

Considering intersectional membership from a Christian perspective means recognizing that new experiences and a plurality of stories impact the interpretation of sacred scripture. The story of science informs a reading of Genesis as a symbolic account of creation. The story of feminism enables us to read the gospels with women as central to the early Jesus movement. The experience of poverty is critical to identifying the life of Jesus as a tool for social justice. But as a reciprocal, mutually interpreting process, the story of scripture should also inform the readings of science, feminism and poverty. The human person is not merely the composition of chemical processes; the values of Genesis intertextually point to this and offer input to science, for example, in the conversation of bioethics. In a similar way, the feminist struggle becomes not the advancement of women at all costs, but informed by the discipleship of equals evidenced in the gospels, the story of Christian feminism extends to embrace the struggle against multiple forms of oppression. The story and values of religion can reciprocally inform the understanding of economics, such that statistics on poverty are not merely a set of figures but are recognized as the intolerable condition of living human beings with an inherent dignity. Communicative exchange among the many stories that shape us helps to deepen and expand the vision of human existence in a complex universe.

This communicative exchange is not only between a religious community and the nonreligious frameworks of philosophy or science, for example. Rather, in the era of globalization, the pluralistic sites we inhabit mean that exchange may take place among different faith perspectives as well. As Christians encounter and learn from their religiously other neighbors, these alternative insights into experience, organizing patterns and sacred stories can help Christians to see new ways of understanding the world. Michael Amaladoss describes the possibilities of such exchange as resources for our shared world. He writes,

> In a situation where believers of different religions share the
> same economic, political, social and cultural structures and

religion is not limited to the private sphere, they must be able to collaborate in the defense and promotion of common human and spiritual values, though each religious group finds motivation and inspiration for such involvement in its own religion.[6]

In our world, persons of different religious communities are related by virtue of the physical proximity of shared space and invested in the promotion of common human values, although distinctively motivated by particular understandings. Amaladoss underscores the need for *ongoing* cooperation in localized contexts. He suggests that we create common human and spiritual values to sustain persons across difference. The emphasis is on how we create them in conversation. In his own words,

> Common human and spiritual values are not based on some presumed natural law common to all or on some abstract rational philosophy considered universally valid. They should evolve from an ongoing conversation between the different religious groups.... There may not be easy solutions, but what is important is that each believer is able to draw on his or her religious resources and tradition and that different religious groups are in an ongoing conversation in fashioning an ever-dynamic consensus.[7]

The distinctive religious traditions offer specific resources from out of which an "ever-dynamic" consensus is forged.

The experiences of being in contact with persons of diverse faiths and hearing the way the world looks through their eyes can influence a person's understanding of the world and his/her own sacred story. In the process of communicative exchange, we are reminded of the variety of ways persons can find orientation in the universe, and see that our paradigm is not the only one to offer suggestions for thinking our way forward. Like the differences between scientific explanation and one grounded in the sacred story of a religion, differences between the explanations of various religious outlooks arise from the distinctive constellation and framework of the particular community. But like the story of science as related to the story of religion, religious stories in contact will not always be compatible on multiple levels. Since we do not see the world through the framework of the other's story, we may find their ideas and claims disorienting. Here we learn from Lindbeck's concern that religious communities share among themselves unsubstitutable memories embedded in the lines of their sacred stories. At times, indeed, we are speaking altogether different languages; we cannot know fully the memories that shape the experience of another.

Again, if we followed Lindbeck's construction of religious identity formulated only on the stories of our sacred scripture, we might have to admit along with him the impossibility of understanding across difference. Yet, because we are adopting a different construction of identity, we might see that when people are shaped by a multiplicity of stories the conditions for conversation across difference are in place. Because our frameworks are created intertextually from out of many stories, while two people might not share the story of their religious community, they may have in common some additional stories. They might share the same story of culture or ethnicity, of profession or generational outlook. They may have in common the story of democracy or feminism. Or as Amaladoss describes, they may simply share a concern for the material reality of common space. Although persons may not view the world through the same religious story, the many facets of identities suggests that they can find a common language in one of the other stories that shape them. Through a shared story, elements of a common language are available through which to communicate. This common story may provide resources also for talking about the particulars of our distinctive sacred story. But in order to share the story of religion, and in order for the stories of the religions to function as resources at the intersection of shared concerns, persons must actually be shaped by the particularities of the story itself. The resources available for shared action originate in the distinctive stories of our traditions.

The story of Christian scripture is one possible site for orientation to the mystery of existence. This story is rooted in history, in the life and ministry of a first-century Jew who committed his adult life to the transformation of his world. This is fundamentally the story of a compassionate human being, whose care for others and love for the mystery he named "God" intertwined in a holistic vision of human well-being and God's care for creation. Living under Roman occupation, Jesus recognized injustice as it was manifest in social, political and religious forms. He saw some of his fellow Jews dehumanized by the oppressive systems of colonial occupation which stole their freedom for the benefit of the Roman Empire. He saw some of his fellow Jews distanced from God by the religious elite whose concepts of purity and legality kept people from participation in the religious life of the community. He saw the poor and disabled doubly dehumanized by both of these systematic oppressions as they could not find physical, spiritual or social well-being under these systems of exclusionary practice.

The story of Jesus of Nazareth is the story of a first-century Jew who saw his religious tradition coopted by material concerns and imprisoned by some religious elites. It is the story of transforming and renewing his inherited tradition so that it might continue to speak to people. While necessarily critical of some of the forms of Judaism in his day, Jesus' ability to assess injustice and the need for transformation was rooted in his profound understanding of God as it had been communicated to him in his Jewish tradition. His understanding of God was shaped by Judaism's affirmation that God has a special care and concern for humanity, that God's will is human well-being and God's presence can be found in the world and in history. Drawing on the traditions of Hebrew Scripture that identify God as Creator, Jesus' affirmations often rested on creation as a source of knowledge about God. As the gospel writers recall a characteristic teaching, Jesus says:

> Look at the birds of the air; they neither sow nor reap nor gather into barns, and yet your heavenly Father feeds them. Are you not of more value than they? [. . .] Consider the lilies of the field how they grow; they neither toil nor spin, yet I tell you, even Solomon in all his glory was not clothed like one of these. But if God so clothes the grass of the field, which is alive today and tomorrow is thrown into the oven, will he not

much more clothe you — you of little faith? (Matt. 6:26–30;
Luke 12:22–31)

Creation reveals that the mysterious source of existence sustains
all beings. Humanity is intimately cared for and wholly wrapped
up in the designs of an awesome universe. The response to this
realization is two-fold. First, Jesus calls here for trust in the source of
creation that he names "God"; second, in other writings of the New
Testament, Jesus calls humanity into participation in the mystery of
existence by extending God's care to the world.

Created by a God whose concern is human well-being and who
attends to the needs of humanity, human beings are called to extend this practice of care and concern in their own lives. This was
Jesus' vision of humanity being called to, experiencing and living in
the "kingdom of God." As Elisabeth Schüssler Fiorenza explains,
Jesus' vision was one that embodied the wholeness God intended
in creation. Those who gathered around Jesus and worked with
him found their life pattern in the welcoming care intended by God
and extended in the world. Schüssler Fiorenza draws attention to
the symbol of the festive meal evidenced in the gospel texts and
which likely reflects the practice of early Christians gathering at
table to experience and celebrate the goodness of God's creation
in food and fellowship. An important dimension of this fellowship
rests in its openness to all, with a special concern for those otherwise marginalized in society. The poor, the sick, the sinner were
welcomed expressly to share at the table and to experience the fundamental goodness of creation and the reality of God's care. This
reality could, at times, only be experienced through the outreach-
ing of neighbor to neighbor. Thus, Jesus' practices of healings and
attention to the outcast made the care of God for humanity an
experiential reality.[8] Jesus' life practice enlivened the kingdom of
God, and those who followed his pattern of practice also brought
about the kingdom in their lives. Embodying the care of God for all
creation, the community that gathered was constructed as a "discipleship of equals" where "first and last" no longer held the currency
that society had given them. The wisdom Jesus embodied, God's
wisdom in the world, did not abide by the definitions of wisdom

embraced by many in the world. This wisdom was hidden from the "wise and intelligent" (Luke 10:21; Matt. 11:25) and made accessible to the uneducated, impure and outcast.

Jesus' wisdom and his vision of the kingdom that emerge from the stories of the gospels have three essential foci: God, others and action. The kingdom that Jesus promotes is understood as "God's kingdom," and his work is understood to be God's own work in the world (e.g., John 5:19). The unfathomable source that brought existence into being continues its work through the life and ministry of Jesus of Nazareth. It is through Jesus' work that humanity aligns with the aims of the incomprehensible God. This vision closely links the mysterious origin of creation and the well-being of creation itself. This is especially true of the well-being of humanity, but is inclusive also of the earth and other dimensions of the created order. While earth, humanity and creation are linked closely to this vision that is the "kingdom of God," this kingdom is often contrasted with the kingdoms of this world. The contrast does not rest on rejecting the things of this world, but in resisting those things that work against the kingdom vision of God's wholeness. The contrast is between the things of God's reign and forces that promote the "anti-reign." From a socio-historical perspective, the original contrast may have been with the kingdom of the Roman Empire and those forces that colluded with the dehumanization it often promoted. Speaking more generally of the New Testament themes, the contrast of God's kingdom is with the concerns and glories of this world, including money, power and status. Reflecting this reversal of wisdom is the story of Jesus calling children to him and using their powerlessness as an example of the humility to which all are called. The text of Matthew's gospel reads:

> "Who is the greatest in the kingdom of heaven?" He called a child, whom he put among them, and said, "Truly I tell you, unless you change and become like children, you will never enter the kingdom of heaven. Whoever becomes humble like this child is the greatest in the kingdom of heaven. Whoever welcomes one such child in my name welcomes me." (Matt. 18:1–5)

It is not the wise and powerful esteemed by this world who issue in the kingdom of God, but the powerless child who holds no status according to the wisdom of the world. Adopting the attitudes and actions of the humble of the world brings about the creation intended by the mysterious source of our existence, brings about the kingdom of God.

In the texts of the canonical gospels, we learn Jesus' vision of true greatness is a reversal of the expectation of conventional wisdom, both in his day and in our own. The call to humility and service echoes throughout the texts:

> "Whoever wants to be first must be last of all and servant of all." (Mark 9:35)

> "Whoever becomes humble like this child is the greatest in the kingdom of heaven." (Matt. 18:4)

> "Whoever welcomes this child in my name welcomes me, and whoever welcomes me welcomes the one who sent me; for the least among you is the greatest." (Luke 9:47–8)

The reign of wholeness is grounded in the human capacity for care of the least among us and solidarity in service to all. Thus, Jesus' kingdom vision is identified with the poor, the poor in spirit, the meek, the merciful, the peacemakers, those falsely accused, those who are hungry, those who are excluded, and those who hunger and thirst for righteousness (Matt. 5:3–11; Luke 6:20–23). Throughout the gospels, his vision is remembered as one that was grounded in love. "I give you a new commandment, that you love one another. Just as I have loved you, you also should love one another. By this everyone will know that you are my disciples" (John 13:34–35). We have the potential to live in a reign of love, wholeness and inclusion, for Jesus indicates that "the kingdom of God is among you" (Luke 17:21).

The wisdom Jesus preached was countercultural or "unconventional" as scholar Marcus Borg describes it; it emerged in contrast to and in conflict with the wisdom of this world.[9] If the wisdom of this world offers violence as an acceptable route to solving our conflicts, the direction to turn the other cheek ran visibly against the grain. If the wisdom of this world holds up success, wealth and social power as the preferred mode of being, Jesus' wisdom seems radically out of place, as the gospel writers describe him spending his time on earth among the outcasts of his day, seeking out not the powerful and popular, but the shunned and broken. The wisdom of the world as Jesus met it also conveyed that the route to God was through religious leaders and exclusive practices of religious piety and purity. Jesus' wisdom sought out the excluded and identified the route to God "not primarily [in] holiness but wholeness."[10] This wholeness was not only preached, but enacted in his life. Those broken in physical, social and mental ways experienced healing in his presence; those marginalized and excluded found human connection and experienced the gratuitous gift of fellowship; those missing some peace and contentment of spirit found wholeness in his vision and his community.

The life that gave rise to the powerful story of Christian scripture, was not a life lived in solitude, and the story as it was lived in history was not the story of Jesus alone. It was a life-story shared by those who gathered and were guided by his vision and lived his story alongside him in the Jesus Movement.[11] He was, as Borg suggests, a "movement initiator" whose vision caught on and captured the hopes and lives of those who journeyed on this earth with him.[12] They too lived this story in history, during the time when Jesus was alive, but also following his death. Through the life and ministry of Jesus of Nazareth, those who followed him saw something of the face of God. The mystery of creation and existence was revealed to them in this powerful and passionate life, lived on behalf of the marginalized and with attention to the restoration of the wholeness of humanity. Through Jesus' compassionate concern, those who followed him experienced firsthand the compassionate concern of the God who created them. They saw something affirmative about the God who is incomprehensible mystery. Schüssler Fiorenza explains what they could affirm: "The Sophia-G*d of Jesus loves all humanity irrespective of ethnic and social links and shows concern for liberation and empowerment of the underprivileged."[13] The Jesus Movement promoted the central idea that our world could be transformed by committing one's life to the new vision of God's kingdom on earth. This was a kingdom of wholeness and fellowship, lived in solidarity with God and others, where the well-being of each person was equally valued and thus special attention was given to the powerless and marginalized. This reign of well-being would enable all people to live fully human lives, secure in their needs, gladdened by the goodness of creation and in a fellowship of equality with all. In continuity with the justice and concern for the poor that runs throughout the Hebrew Scriptures, Jesus' wisdom and his kingdom vision was of a world where humans were able to thrive because all persons held to the values of truth, justice, closeness to God and goodness to one another. The idea that in the kingdom of God, "the righteous will shine like the sun" (Matt. 13:43), echoes the words of revelation spoken to Daniel, "Those who are wise shall shine like the brightness of the sky and those who lead many to righteousness, like the stars forever and ever" (Dan. 12:3). Drawing on the story of his ancient Jewish tradition, Jesus re-presented this story to enliven all who would listen.

But countercultural wisdoms and alternative lifestyles that gather momentum and strength in solidarity are characteristically threatening to those who benefit from the conventional wisdom that structures a world where power, wealth and prestige bring social and material gain. Jesus' refusal to participate in conventional wisdom, threatening as it was to those in power, also led to his death. He would not give in to the temptations to abandon the countercultural commitment to an alternative world, even when his life was threatened. Reflected in the episodes of the gospels, it was the wisdom of a world where religious systems are used to mask economic profit and greed that raised the eyebrows of suspicion at Jesus' outrage with the selling and buying in the Temple. It was the wisdom of a world where religious territorialism and intolerance is justified as God's will that put Jesus to death. It was the wisdom of a world where political power is threatened by alternative visions, and violence is used to solve conflicts that put Jesus to death. It was the wisdom of a world where justice is often corrupted by bribery, cover-up and influence, and where the law is often on the side of the privileged that put Jesus to death. Jesus of Nazareth refused to play by the rules set by the wisdom of his world. In succession with the prophets before him who spoke out against the wisdom of this world, he spoke out with his life.[14]

It would seem that Jesus' story is the story of the human condition writ large: a story of wisdom and righteousness being repaid by cruelty and betrayal; the story of a champion of the forgotten and the broken crushed by the power of the wisdom of this world. As Jesus hangs on the cross, disdained by his religious "others" and put to death at the hands of Judea's Roman occupiers, the moral of the story is this: challenge the wisdom of this world, the wisdom of power and violence and greed, and you will suffer, you will be killed. It would be no surprise if those who had lived this story with Jesus and saw the utopian possibilities of his vision were demoralized by the cross. If the one who lived so according to righteousness and the wisdom of God falls at the hands of the power of this world, what hope can there be?

If the story ended there, Christians across the centuries might be a miserable bunch. Christians would somberly take on the role of scapegoats for the powers that rule under conventional wisdom. There would be no hope that Jesus' unconventional wisdom held any power at all. But the story does not end with the cross. The story of each gospel does not even pause to consider those who followed Jesus as being dispirited or confused. The story continues. Mary of Magdala and her companions carry on the story in the gospel texts when they witness the vindication of the resurrection (John 20:11, Matt. 28:1, Mark 16:1, Luke 24:10). God does not stand on the side of those who embrace the conventional wisdom of violence, marginalization and injustice. In the resurrection event, the community of the Jesus Movement experienced Jesus' presence among them and realized God's commitment to those who commit their lives to God's will. For it is the central faith affirmation of Christians that Jesus' story did not end in his death but that his story continues as witness and hope that the kingdom of God might still be a reality. As Jon Sobrino explains, "In a world such as ours, full of lies and cruelty, martyrs tell us that truth and love, firmness and faithfulness, and love to the end are possible. And that is good news."[15] The good news of Jesus Christ lies firmly in his commitment to the unconventional wisdom of the kingdom in his life and in his death.

This good news is confirmed as God's news in the resurrection. As Sobrino recalls the description of Jesus Christ witnessed in the New Testament, "The risen Lord, then, is Jesus of Nazareth, who proclaimed the Kingdom of God to the poor, denounced the powerful, was persecuted and sentenced, and throughout maintained a radical fidelity to the will of God and a radical trust in this same God, whom he called Father." He goes on to reflect,

> This description of the risen Lord is decisive for clarifying what the resurrection of Jesus reveals of God. God has raised the one who has lived in this way and who was crucified for doing so. God has raised an innocent one and done justice to the victim. Jesus' resurrection is then not only a symbol of God's omnipotence ... but is presented as the defense God makes of the life of the Righteous One and of the victims.[16]

In the life and death of Jesus of Nazareth and the experience of resurrection, Jesus' followers were able to affirm certain elements about the one whom they named "God." The incomprehensible source of existence and Creator whose ways are unfathomable holds a special care for the outcast and desires the well-being of all humanity. The ways of God are indeed inscrutable and will not be found within the wisdom of this world, but they are, in part, known through the life and ministry of Jesus of Nazareth. God's wisdom is no longer wholly beyond the reach of human understanding, rather, God's wisdom is made a living reality in Jesus Christ.

In the framework of the Christian story, Jesus' life and ministry are intimately linked to human salvation. What it meant to find salvation in the life and person of Jesus, among the first Christians, appears to have been necessarily connected with their own life pattern and practice of action. In a world such as ours where burdens abound, Jesus calls those who follow him to take on the easy yoke of gentleness and humility of heart. "Come to me, all you that are weary and are carrying heavy burdens and I will give you rest. Take my yoke upon you, and learn from me; for I am gentle and humble in heart, and you will find rest for your souls. For my yoke is easy, and my burden is light" (Matt. 11:28–30). When these words are put on the lips of Jesus, the author of the text is envisioning Jesus as

God's own wisdom present in the world. For these words echo the words of Wisdom as she is personified in the Hebrew Scriptures in, for example, Sirach 24:19 and 51:23. As Schüssler Fiorenza describes, "Sophia [Wisdom] is the personification of G*d's saving activity in the world."[17] God saves, then, through patterns of humility and gentleness; Jesus provides that pattern in his life.

To experience Jesus as savior was to follow in his life-giving practice. In the letter to the Philippians, for example, Paul links the proclamation of the name of Jesus to the continuation of Jesus' care for others and humble service. His audience is encouraged to "work out your own salvation" by following the practice of Jesus; and through that to "shine like stars in the world" (Phil. 2:12 and 15). In Paul's letters, Jesus' name is linked to salvation and to the self-giving practice patterned on Jesus. Through actions of humble service with the interest of others in mind, God's salvific power courses through the community. Similarly when we read the story of Acts, we recognize that salvation for the author of Luke-Acts is a "restoration to wholeness" with "the universality of salvation available in Christ for all human beings who turn to him."[18] The community continues the active healing that was characteristic of Jesus' own ministry, and defends its actions saying,

> Rulers of the people and elders, if we are questioned today because of a good deed done to someone who was sick and are asked how this man has been healed, let it be known to all of you, and to all the people of Israel, that this man is standing before you in good health by the name of Jesus Christ of Nazareth, whom you crucified, whom God raised from the dead. This Jesus is the stone that was rejected by you, the builders; it has become the cornerstone. There is salvation in no one else, for there is no other name under heaven given among mortals by which we must be saved. (Acts 4:8–12).

What it means to proclaim Jesus as Savior in this biblical context, is to hold him up as witness to the healing power of God.[19] In these biblical declarations, the proclamation of Jesus' salvific efficacy is specifically related to the continuation of the healing and humility of Jesus himself.

And so, after his death, the communities of the Jesus Movement continued his vision emboldened by the vindication God had shown to the righteous one. These women and men set out to pattern their lives on the life of Jesus of Nazareth. As Paul's letter to the Philippians reflects, they were encouraged toward "whatever is true, whatever is honorable, whatever is just, whatever is pure, whatever is pleasing, whatever is commendable" (Phil. 4:8). And again in a letter to the community at Thessalonica when he writes,

> Be at peace among yourselves. And we urge you, beloved, to admonish the idlers, encourage the fainthearted, help the weak, be patient with all of them. See that none of you repays evil for evil, but always seek to do good to one another and to all. Rejoice always, pray without ceasing, give thanks in all circumstances; for this is the will of God in Christ Jesus for you. Do not quench the Spirit. Do not despise the words of the prophets, but test everything; hold fast to what is good; abstain from every form of evil. (1 Thess. 5:13–22)

In the person of Jesus of Nazareth and the experience of the risen Christ, the early Christian community witnessed the real presence of God's relatedness to humanity. Persons recognized the power of ultimate reality coursing through this life, revealing Godself in and through the life practice of healing and illuminative teachings of this first-century Jew. In retelling the story of their experience of God's revelation in Christ, the earliest witnesses sought also to shape a practice of following Jesus and to create a community of affiliative belonging. As Francis Schüssler Fiorenza says, "The Gospels are narratives about Jesus *and* stories of Christian identity. They do not just relate the story of Jesus, they also spell out the beginning of the Christian story of discipleship."[20] In the Easter experience, the continued presence of the risen Christ — his power of healing and revelation of God's goodness — coursed also through the community itself. Experiencing this in none other than Jesus Christ, his role in relating persons to the mystery of existence was central.

The pattern of linking salvation and practice is evidenced also in 1 Timothy 2:4–6, where the author emphasizes God as the Savior of humanity, who works in and through Jesus Christ as mediator.

For there is one God; there is also one mediator between God and humankind, Christ Jesus, himself human, who gave himself a ransom for all — this was attested at the right time. (1 Tim. 2:4–6)

The author of this letter underscores again the "self-donative pattern of Jesus' existence"[21] that is emphasized in his self-giving action on behalf of others in this salvific proclamation. In the story of Christians, none other than Jesus of Nazareth holds the life-fulfilling practice to follow. Exegete Luke Timothy Johnson notes that salvation in the context of the letter to Timothy "is less about a future destiny ('eternal life'), than about present location. Salvation has a specific sociological referent: God wills all people to belong to the people God is forming in the world."[22] The sociological referent in the New Testament sources describes the end for which humans were created ("salvation") not in other-worldly terms, but as a present reality to which humans are called. Collapsing the dualism of this world/the next, salvation, as a posture of relatedness and participation in the holy mystery, is engaged precisely in the context of human historicity and locatedness. Whoever/whatever God is, human persons are made aware of God's mystery through that which is available to them — their experience in this world.

Just as our identities are forged in contact with others, so too the transcendence of salvation ought to be understood in relation to our social world, that is, in relationship to other human beings. As Gustavo Gutiérrez so clearly describes, "Salvation is not something otherworldly, in regard to which the present life is merely a test. Salvation — the communion of human beings with God and among themselves — is something which embraces all human reality [and] transforms it...."[23] Orientations to God in salvation are part and parcel of our experience in the world and include solidarity with other human beings.[24] If God is envisioned as that which calls humanity into being and toward ever greater becoming, then human relatedness to God takes place whenever and wherever humans are enabled toward being and becoming. We foster God's presence in the world not only through our own transcendence and becoming, but also in fostering the being and becoming of our neighbor. This is the pattern identifiable in Jesus' life. This is salvation. As Ada María Isasi-Díaz writes,

> Salvation is gratuitously given by God; it flows from the very essence of God: love. Salvation is worked out through the love between God and each human being and among human beings. . . . Therefore, love sets in motion and sustains the on-going act of God's salvation in which each person necessarily participates, since love requires, per se, active involvement of those who are in relationship. Our participation in the act of salvation is what we refer to as liberation. It consists of our work to transform the world.[25]

Salvation does not reside solely on the divine side of the human-divine relationship, but through active attention to solidarity and liberative relations to others, humans are agents in co-creating salvation.

In the Christian story, none other than Jesus of Nazareth provides the pattern for salvation in solidarity and wholeness. And, the story of God's unrepeatable presence in the person of Jesus Christ is unique insofar as it bears a particularity. The story is understood to be connected to the historical person of Jesus of Nazareth — unique as each of us are unique in history. Further, the story bears a particularity in the specific memories of the earliest communities who molded their lives on the life and witness of Jesus. As a testimony to God's salvific presence to humanity, the Christian witness to Jesus Christ also forms the framework for understanding discipleship that shapes the self-identity and practice of the Christian community. The life-giving orientation to God through Christ is found in the lines of the Christian story: in the healing praxis, ministry of justice and discipleship of equals patterned after the life and teaching of Jesus Christ. A life lived through the lines of this story is a life molded on the self-sacrificing struggle for human wholeness witnessed in the person of Jesus and remembered by his earliest followers. The stories of Jesus provide orientation of discipleship for the affiliative community of Christians, where the commitment to Jesus Christ can be understood as a commitment to the God whom Christ reveals.[26]

It is through the story of Jesus of Nazareth that Christians make affirmations about God. This story orients them to the mystery of existence by recalling Jesus' life and by sketching what our lives would look like if lived through the lines of the narrative. The story of Christian scripture organizes the data of reality to affirm that God cares for human well-being, and that humans are called to carry on that care by reaching out to others. The ultimate answer to the question, why are we here, is offered in the care shown to the outcast and the kingdom of God humanity is called to create. We are brought into existence to co-create the kingdom of God — a social reality where none are hungry, none are broken and none are outcast. The lines of our sacred story say that this kingdom of God is a real possibility and that humans are called to create it. Through the story, Christians affirm that nearness to the Creator of the universe and alignment with the mysterious source of the existence can be found by patterning one's life on the life and ministry of Jesus.

The story which shapes Christian experience in the world is, in a very real sense, not one story but many stories woven together over time. It is rooted in the life and ministry of an individual in history and those who came to know him and to share his vision. But as the story was retold in a variety of contexts in different locations and at different times, new ways of understanding the story and telling the story emerged. The story that emerges from the gospels is a story with multiple layers. The gospel writers rewove the story of Judaism with the new experience of Jesus of Nazareth; so too did they weave themselves and their context into this story. Mark's identification of Jesus as the suffering servant allowed him to weave into the life and ministry of Jesus a special concern for the endurance of suffering. This was because Mark's community itself is believed to have been experiencing the suffering of a new community of Christians under Roman persecution. Matthew's gospel was written to Jewish-Christians trying to understand their continued relationship to Judaism after the fall of the Temple, the holy site of identity and community. Jesus is seen as the new Temple, the continuation of Israel par excellence. The good news of Jesus' life and ministry is woven together with the questions of Jewish identity in the late first century. Luke's gospel retells the story of Jesus attentive to the concerns of non-Jews and thus draws out the dimensions of his life and ministry that might appeal to a wider Gentile audience. John's gospel is written with a sophisticated philosophical and theological view that tells the story of Jesus through this lens, again because of the audience in mind. So too, every theological reflection from Jesus' day to our own. Each has been woven through with the particular context and location, the concerns and the horizon of the author him or herself. Through the many retellings and reweavings of the story we gather a collective portrait of the life which stands at the heart of the story: the life and ministry of Jesus of Nazareth.

Today, I continue retelling the story of Jesus of Nazareth attentive to my own context of religious pluralism. The context in which we find ourselves in the twenty-first century is one where we are increasingly in contact with persons of diverse faith traditions. We seek strategies for co-existence in our divided yet shrinking world. As persons of diverse faiths become our co-workers, friends, neighbors and life-partners, we also want to investigate their role in our ongoing understanding of the mystery of existence which Christians name "God." As we seek these understandings, we carry with us the heritage of Christian participation in colonial oppression and domination of the "other" in the name of religion. The idea that "salvation" is the monopoly of the Christian tradition and that there is "no salvation outside the Church" has been wielded as a weapon of oppression and the erasure of "otherness." The suggestion that Christians alone know God or that only Christian affirmations about God are true have established barriers between Christians and persons of other faiths. Both have been the cause of division and arrogance. Thus, I seek strategies of solidarity in relationships of equality and respect to heal the fractures Christians have created in history.

Following the hermeneutical method of Elisabeth Schüssler Fiorenza, I look to the New Testament as paradigmatic remembrances of the Jesus Movement which called forth a way of life. When asking how to live the call of discipleship in the context of contemporary religious pluralism, I turn to the text as a lens that might provide a liberating vision on which to pattern a Christian response. This approach to the text understands the Bible, "not as conglomeration of doctrinal propositions or proofs, not as historical-factual transcripts, but as the model of Christian faith and life."[27] A pastoral-theological paradigm for understanding the resource of Christian scripture recognizes that the interpretation of the text will be shaped by the context of our theological concern. Just as the gospels were written for certain communities and molded to address particular concerns, so too today's reading of the story of scripture as guide to life and action is informed by contemporary concerns. For the gospel writers, "the concrete pastoral situation of the community determines selection, transmission, and creation of the biblical tradition;"[28] so too the framework of our story relies on our concrete historical situation to select central texts to guide thought and behavior.

Today's context is conditioned by the reality of religious difference. Christians are shaped by the story of Christ, yet they increasingly encounter others who have been shaped by the stories of other religious traditions. Christians are also haunted by the dangerous memory of past encounters with religious difference where Christian power was not the healing practice of Jesus of Nazareth, but rather the domination and oppression reflected in the conventional wisdom of this world. The New Testament offers an understanding of "salvation" as the restoration of wholeness engaged in the context of our world. The world we find ourselves in is one all too often divided on the basis of religion. Religious identity, intertwined as it has been with imperialism and cultural erasure, has often been the cause of brokenness. Recognizing this reality and allowing our context to shape the reading of scripture, we read Jesus' sermon on the plain in a quite different way. Luke's text reads: "Blessed are you when people hate you, and when they exclude you, revile you and defame you on account of the Son of Man. Rejoice in that day and leap for joy, for surely your reward is great in heaven; for that is what their ancestors did to the prophets" (Luke 6:22–3). As Luke Timothy Johnson suggests, the sermon recognizes the blessedness of those who suffer from attitudes (reviling/hatred), actions (exclusion) and speech (defamation) by which others marginalize them.[29] In the traditional reading of this text, of course, those who are persecuted on account of the Son of Man are interpreted to be Christians excluded for their commitment to Christ.[30] But as pastoral-theological resources, could we not read the experience of the non-Christian into these lines? Are not our neighbors of other faiths often hated on account of Jesus, the Son of Man? Have they not been excluded and reviled and defamed, in the name of Jesus of Nazareth? New experiences and new contexts allow fresh meanings to leap from the pages of scripture. And the history of Christian exclusion and persecution of other faiths in the name of salvation and the name of Jesus Christ certainly begs that we reconsider the lines of our story haunted by this memory and bearing its responsibility.

Accepting that Christians were intimately engaged in breaking the religious identity of the other, we might acknowledge a responsibility for healing precisely *this* brokenness and restoring the world to wholeness. In our current world where religious identities continue to be the source of division, we might seek a restoration of wholeness among persons of diverse faiths. Salvation is "worked out" in solidarity with the religiously other. Recognizing the need for salvation in the restoration to wholeness of our broken world, I return to the sacred story of the Christian tradition, seeking the pattern of discipleship to follow in this process. Searching the scriptures, I find Luke chapter 10. It reads,

> Just then a lawyer stood up to test Jesus. "Teacher," he said, "what must I do to inherit eternal life?" Jesus said to him, "What is written in the law? What do you read there?" The lawyer answered, *"You shall love the Lord your God with all your heart, and with all your soul, and with all your strength, and with all your mind; and your neighbor as yourself."* And Jesus said to him, "You have given the right answer; do this, and you will live." (Luke 10:25–28)

In this first-century witness to the life and ministry of Jesus of Nazareth, the Teacher describes a path to life that is marvelously simple, yet profound. He suggests that a life of abundance, the inheritance of eternal life (or "salvation") is rooted, quite simply, in love. All dimensions of the human person — the emotional (heart), the rational (mind), the spiritual (soul), the physical (strength) — are bound up in a "centered act" of relationship between the individual and the divine.[31] Loving God with this intensity and focus, the dynamic love between self and God overflows to envelope also the neighbor. This brings life.

Yet, like the lawyer of the first century, the twenty-first century reader might inadvertently calculate precisely to whom this neighborly love ought to extend. The story of Luke continues. Just as Jesus affirms that life is found in loving God and loving one's neighbor as oneself, the lawyer asks Jesus, "And who is my neighbor?" (Luke 10:29) Jesus replies with a parable: "A man was going down from Jerusalem to Jericho and fell into the hands of robbers...." In the story of the Good Samaritan, the man who is left half-dead in the road is aided not by his kinsmen or those of pious occupations, but by a foreigner moved with compassion. From the story, the reader is called to see the neighbor in this good Samaritan.

The parable that answers the question — "And who is my neighbor?" — is significant for our concerns because of the neighbor who Jesus identifies. From the standpoint of the first-century lawyer, the Samaritan would have appeared as one who was socially and religiously other, held suspect because the Samaritan's religious practices situated him as neither Jew nor Gentile.[32] But it is precisely *this* "other" who stands as representative of the neighbor who is to be enveloped in the love that flows between oneself and God. When asked the most fundamental question of existence, Jesus answers that in order to live we must love the neighbor-who-is-other.

If we are applying Jesus' vision to our twenty-first-century world, with the resources we have and the historical precedents we have seen, we envision the practice of loving the neighbor-who-is-other in a distinctive way. We think especially about the religiously other neighbor and the relationships Christians have fostered over the centuries. We call to mind the friendships fostered in the ancient world, when new Christians considered their relationships with friends and family members of the Jewish and Greek traditions a distinctive part of their own identity. We remember Christians sharing meals and accepting invitations to do so in the "other's" house of worship, as indicated in Paul's letters to the Corinthians and Romans on the issue of eating meat in Greek social contexts. In these memories, there is a sense that "otherness" is often found among the familiar. Friends, family members, colleagues may see the world through the lens of another faith. Like these Jewish and Greek predecessors, contemporary Christians might engage in the dialogue of life and shape their identity in conversation with people of diverse faiths.

Loving the neighbor-who-is-other is also the call to Christians who do not have family members or friends of a different faith. Like Roberto de Nobili and Matteo Ricci, we may need to seek out those who are other in creative and committed ways. But many of us will not need to travel halfway around the world to encounter religious otherness; increasingly, our world is characterized by religious difference in close contact. Learning from de Nobili and Ricci, however, encourages us to encounter, engage with and learn from the distinctive lifestyles of our neighbors. It is not sufficient to tolerate difference in our communities, but as de Nobili and Ricci model, our relationships should be ones of real engagement in shared lifestyles with our neighbors of other faiths. The chance encounter is not enough. The approaches of de Nobili and Ricci encourage us to seek out the religiously other neighbor and foster ongoing relationships where discussion and exchange can take place. With established relationships, we are able to participate in the dialogue of theological exchange that allows us to recognize a distinctive perspective in other faiths.

Yet another precedent from history encourages us to draw near to the religiously other neighbor in response to Jesus' call in Luke 10. This precedent is the dialogue of social action patterned on the life-practice of Jesus and evidenced in the life of Bartolomé de Las Casas. When Las Casas developed relationships with the religiously other in Latin America, he was moved to defend their humanity against the Spanish-Christians who rejected the encounter with otherness altogether. Las Casas insisted that the differences found in the native people did not erase their complex humanity and defended them against the acts of injustice perpetrated in the name of Spain and Christendom. The dialogue of social action can take place in our own contexts when we see that our religiously other neighbors are discriminated against on the basis of their faith tradition. We are called to pattern our response on the life-pattern of Jesus and to seek the well-being of our neighbors regardless of their religious tradition. The dialogue of social justice is also manifest in shared struggles for social justice across traditional lines. In the shared practice of social action, we work alongside our neighbors of other faiths for a more just world, recognizing that their participation may be informed explicitly by their distinctive faith perspective. In the shared struggles, we might learn more about what motivates them from the perspective of their faith.

In all of these approaches to loving the neighbor, we want to draw near to the neighbor-who-is-other without erasing their otherness. For if we erase otherness, we are no longer drawing near to him or her who is different, but are seeking to draw near to sameness. We do not want to posit an imagined sameness because that would eliminate the very distinctiveness that makes this neighbor "other." Rather, we seek to maintain the differences while drawing near in relationships of solidarity and engagement. As we have seen, we can draw near to the other precisely by recognizing the many facets of our identities. We draw on the fact that each of our neighbors is not only religiously other, but has an identity constructed at the intersection of geographical location, political affiliation, race, class, gender, nationality, ethnicity, profession, sexual orientation, and so forth, just as we do. With the multiple aspects of who we are, we find dimensions of ourselves that we share with our religious others. It is the overlap in our webs of identity that draws us into relationships of simultaneous sameness and difference. Although we may not share the sacred stories of our neighbors, the multiplicity of stories that shape us provides resources for solidarity. We can draw on this multiplicity in order to find sites of similarity through which to communicate. Recognizing his/her multiplicity, we join in relationship without erasing religious particularity in the process. We draw near to our religiously other neighbor to embrace him/her in the life-giving pattern of salvific relationship.

With the resources of feminist patterns of thinking about identity and encouraged by the dangerous memories of history, we want to draw near to the religiously other neighbor by recognizing the over-lap of our multifaceted identities. As Christians, we do this guided by the memory of Jesus' direction to love the neighbor-who-is-other and through that love to find the salvation that is the fullness of life. We affirm that God is known in and through the life pattern and practice of Jesus Christ, and so seek to live our lives directed by his witness in the New Testament. When we follow this particular directive — to love the neighbor-who-is-other — we might envision that there are even deeper reasons why we are directed to envelope the religiously other in our salvific relationship. Perhaps they might draw us ever closer to the incomprehensible mystery that is God.

In reading the gospel texts from the perspective of religious plu-ralism, we see the possible Christian patterns of action in embracing our neighbors of other faiths in the love that flows between oneself and God. The question that completes this theological reflection is — why? What can the religiously other neighbor add to this life-giving relationship? One way to answer this is to see the otherness of the other as an indispensable vehicle for recognizing God's infinite incomprehensibility. Through the otherness of the other — uncon-trollable and beyond our understanding — we are brought back to the fundamental affirmation in the Christian tradition: namely, that who God is surpasses all our capacity for understanding. Here we bring back together the elements of affirmation and incomprehen-sibility, whose balance is central to the Christian faith tradition. Emphatically we affirm that Jesus Christ brings us close to the in-comprehensible mystery we name "God." Indeed, in the structure of our story, in the lines of our sacred narrative, it is Jesus of Nazareth alone who brings us to the life-giving relationship that is "salva-tion." There is none other in whom lepers, outcasts and broken ones find healing. It is in none other than his name that those who follow him can carry on his salvific practice. It is through Jesus alone that persons find the life-giving ways of relating to God and others. Within the bounds of the New Testament, the sacred text which shapes communities of Christians, Jesus *is* the sole mediator of salvation. But we recognize also that there are other stories. In the stories of other communities, in the lines of their narratives the incomprehensible mystery may be witnessed in different ways.

While Christians model their orientation to the mystery of existence in the hope and memory of Jesus of Nazareth, they can also recognize the multiple stories of diverse religious communities. The real presence of God in Jesus witnessed in the early Christian community and reflected in the life-shaping testimonies of the New Testament need not rule out additional communities experiencing God's presence and orienting themselves to the incomprehensible mystery through different means. Human orientation to the complex context of existence is not of a singular form, but can be framed and lived in a multiplicity of ways — a central insight of Lindbeck's cultural-linguistic model. Our stories shape us to understand and experience the world in particular ways. It is the concepts made available through our particular stories that afford us distinct ways of understanding the world and our way forward within that world.

Diverse frameworks and communities of affiliation that include the diversity of religious communities also afford unique relationships to the mysterious source of existence. This diversity is neither an aberration nor a sad reflection on human limitedness, but rather, reflects precisely the nature of God's overflowing abundance that sustains multiple and distinct relationships of human fulfillment.[33] Different understandings of the reality of God mirror the traditional Christian affirmation of God's overabundant knowability. The reality of God is an excess which cannot be contained in the vessel of the human mind. Incomprehensibility "follows from the essential infinity of God which makes it impossible for a finite created intellect to exhaust the possibility of knowledge and truth contained in this absolute fullness of being."[34] Like Teresa of Avila's metaphor of the sponge which cannot contain the reality of the divinity, or Roberto de Nobili's image of the pot that is incapable of containing the fullness of knowledge of God, the Christian tradition has affirmed that God's incomprehensibility arises from overabundance rather than absence. Incomprehensibility follows from the "infinity of [God's] unlimited and pure being"[35] in the contemplation of which the human mind *overflows*.

Karl Rahner has described the process of human knowing as one that can bring about an awareness of the infinite mystery of God. In each act of knowing or learning, the human person goes beyond the limits of what one presently knows and into the context of an infinite extension into the unknown. By comprehending the known object and considering it within one's reference system, one is immediately confronted with the limitless possibility of knowledge. The limitlessness which confronts the knower itself cannot be comprehended. This incomprehensibility which governs understanding and is the context of limitless possibility cannot be placed within the system of referents. It is an infinite context that makes possible both knowledge of finite things and the unlimited potential of human knowing; the infinite unknown is the precondition for all knowing. Encountering the infinite unknown affords persons an awareness of the holy mystery that Christians name "God."

Encountering the unknown in the religious tradition of the other brings us to an awareness of the infinite unknown, the ultimate mystery, which governs all knowing. Recognizing what we do not know about the life, hopes, practices, experiences and aspirations of the other reminds us of the limitless possibilities for knowledge. In the presence of these "others," in learning from the perspectives of people of other faiths, we are offered the opportunity to participate in the unlimited growth of knowledge. And it is only in the presence of the unknown that the growth of knowledge can take place.

For Rahner, the fundamental encounter with God was not only related to the human projects of knowing. As the human person participates in life and continues the process of growth and transcendence into ever-greater becoming, he or she is fundamentally oriented to the boundless range of possibilities contained in the ever-receding horizon of existence. He or she is opened up to the absolute fullness of being. In the process of transcendence, the human person experiences the "overwhelming feeling" of something greater than him/herself which sustains the process of growth and indeed the entire context of existence. For Rahner, this is the "overwhelming experience of God as ever greater."[36] The unlimited possibility for human becoming opens up before each human person and gives witness to the infinite context of growth and transcendence that Rahner names God.

Drawing on Rahner's suggestion, we might see the gospel directive of Luke 10 (to love the religiously other neighbor) as a new variety of experiences that might open us up to transcendence and ever-greater becoming. It is not only when we learn something new about our religiously other neighbor, but when we reach out in relationships of love, we create something new of ourselves. The new possibilities for friendship and love, for knowledge and growth can be embodied in new ways of relating to persons who intersect with our life path. If God is understood as the infinite source of newness and as the infinite horizon of growth and transcendence, Christians can come to an awareness of God through the experience of people other faiths.

When Rahner describes mystery or the infinite unknown as the prerequisite for all knowing, and the limitless horizon outside the self as a necessary condition for becoming, he is describing difference as *the* constitutive element for human participation in the inexhaustible source of existence that is God. That which we are not — God — is the necessary condition for our becoming. Similarly, that which we are not — in the world around us and others we encounter — allows us opportunities to grow beyond our present selves. Difference serves the essential function of opening us up to the vast possibilities for growth and encounter with God in a concrete way since the recognition of God is present to us precisely in the context of our world. It is only by being confronted with the unknown that the human person can self-reflexively become aware of the infinite possibility that opens up before him or her.

As we have seen, one way scholars of religion have described this in the encounter of religious otherness is through the metaphor of the "comparative mirror." As Rita Gross explains, "by really looking into the comparative mirror, we will undoubtedly find many [religious] alternatives that we would be unlikely to imagine on our own."[37] The fruitful exchange among persons of diverse religious perspectives could provide for richer understandings of human religiousness. Casting the encounter theologically, we see that the resources of "difference" open us up to new ways of understanding transcendence toward God and relationship with one another. As we ongoingly recreate our process of transcendence toward the ever-receding horizon of existence, it is only through contact with difference that we see the infinite potential for becoming. Difference is an essential feature that allows for change in growth and transcendence. It is through growth and transcendence that we open ourselves radically to the source of all being that Christians name "God." The newness of knowledge is found only in the unknown, the newness of love is found precisely as we extend outside of ourselves. In the presence of the religious other, when we recognize his or her genuine difference, we are brought to an awareness of that which we are not. We are brought to an awareness of the limitlessness of human possibilities, and perhaps we are brought to an awareness of the mysterious reality of God.

This is why we would not want to erase the otherness of the other in rejecting their distinctiveness (as exclusivists do) or erasing otherness in sameness (as inclusivists and pluralists do). If difference serves the essential function of opening us further to the overabundant mystery of God, then the otherness of the other needs to be safeguarded as a precious gift and opportunity for growth. At the same time, we need to be able to learn from this otherness, which means our differences cannot be all that we have in the encounter (as particularists have framed it). It is our hybrid identities that allow us to draw near to the religiously other neighbor without erasing his/her particularity in the process. While not sharing in the characteristics of our neighbor's religion, we might share other features on which we make connections of conversation. In the process of finding these commonalties, we might have the opportunity to glimpse the incomprehensible mystery as it is seen through their eyes. This glimpse is a precious gift that we may not fully understand, but which reminds us of the incomprehensibility of God.

In considering religious difference as part and parcel of our experience of the mystery of God, we are taking seriously the Christian affirmation of God's universality as the source of all creation, the source of all humanity. In all the dimensions of who we are — rational, emotional, physical, spiritual and more — in all our particularity, humans are the self-communication of God. Taking this seriously, we are reminded of Rahner's words that "really and radically *every* person must be understood as the event of a supernatural self-communication of God."[38] The ultimate reality that is the source of all that is, and the end of all that will be, creates existence as a self-communication of God's own dynamic being. All of creation exists as God's self-communication in grace. As humans participate in the ongoing life of the universe, through the infinite processes of knowledge, will and love, God's self-communication, God's own being is brought into being in the world. This self-communication is in an endlessly diverse particularity. God dwells as the innermost dynamism not only of Christians, but of all persons. In the gospel directive of Luke 10, the self-communication of God in the religiously other is taken up into one's own love relationship to God.

Thus, in addition to valuing the other for how their difference might transform us and open us up to the source of complexity that is God, the other brings us closer to that source of complexity in an even more intimate way — by participating in it. As a self-communication of God, each individual partakes also in "the mysterious character of God."[39] In Rahner's explanation,

> . . . all beings are inscrutable and unfathomable, because they are creatures. Since they are the *result* of the creative knowledge of God their reality and objective truth has such infinite ramifications, essential to an adequate knowledge of them, that comprehensive knowledge of even the tiniest of them is possible only to God. . . .[40]

We cannot know or understand all dimensions of our religiously other neighbors, even as we draw near to them in relationship. But their complexity and unfathomability might be part of the mysterious aspect of God's self-communication in them. As spirit sharing in God's being, the human person shares in God's nature and therefore also in incomprehensibility. The experience of *unknowing* which one encounters in the other, opens one up to the radical complexity and infinite possibility which is God. The "other" participates in the complexity of God and points beyond themselves to the limitless mystery. Recognizing that the unknown brings us to an awareness of the limitless "holy mystery," we might read religious pluralism as a gift which affords us an ever-greater awareness of the mystery and complexity of God.

The gift of religious difference need not be looked upon as a peripheral element for theological thinking. Instead, the engagement with otherness and the experience of unknowing can be at the heart of Christian practice. In the theological tradition of Christian thought, God's overabundance may be glimpsed in the world, but is also seen as an essential characteristic of God encountered in salvation. As Rahner writes,

> The incomprehensibility of God should not then be regarded as a distant reality, for it increases rather than diminishes in the vision of God, in which alone it becomes an inescapable event. It does not describe the remnants of something which, sadly, remains unknown, but rather points to the immediate object of the experience of God in heaven, an object which is present in the mind overflowing with the fullness of God's self-communication.[41]

Thus, it is not the case that we cannot know God simply because of our limited abilities as creatures bound in time and space. Even in the fullness of salvation, in the very presence of God, the human mind cannot encompass what there is to know of God. But this is not seen as a sad reflection on humanity nor a fault in the relationship between Creator and creature. Rather, as Thomas Aquinas explains, ultimate human fulfillment resides in coming to know God as a process that never ends. In Aquinas's vision of eternal life, we are fulfilled not in finally comprehending God, but in the ongoing wonder that is the human posture of relatedness to God. Sustaining this never-ending process of wonder is the overabundance of God which makes God incomprehensible mystery to the human person.

If beatitude and ultimate human fulfillment are characterized as wonder in God's presence, then ever-new perspectives on the mystery of God might constitute the ultimate human experience of salvation. Christians affirm that they have come to know God through the life and story of Jesus of Nazareth. How might our wonder about God be increased through the encounter and exchange with our religiously other neighbor? Difference and distinctive insights of the various faith traditions might, in fact, be the key to human fulfillment in the never-ending coming to know of God. God is the incomprehensible mystery of overabundance whose reality might be reflected in the stories and experiences of our neighbors of other faiths. In this way of thinking, it is the very distinctiveness and particularity of the other — his or her religious "otherness" — which is seen as an invaluable resource for an ever-broadening vision of the mystery of human existence and the mystery which Christians call "God." In this world, as well as the next, we engage with our neighbors of other faiths and are given the opportunity for the fullness of human happiness in the infinite process of coming to know the mysterious, incomprehensible reality of God.

NOTES

Chapter One / Theological Resources

1. Pseudo-Dionysius, "The Divine Names," chapter 1, in *Pseudo-Dionysius: The Complete Works,* trans. Colm Luibheid (New York: Paulist Press, 1987), 98.

2. Thomas Aquinas, *Summa Theologica,* I.I Question 2, Article 1, trans. Anton Pegis (New York: Random House, 1945), 19.

3. Karl Rahner, "Book of God — Book of Human Beings," *Theological Investigations,* vol. 22, trans. Joseph Donceel (New York: Crossroad, 1991), 215.

4. Pseudo-Dionysius, *Divine Names,* 55.

5. Gregory of Nyssa, *Contra Eunomius,* vol. 1, 682, p. 222 (18–24), as quoted in Deirdre Carabine, *The Unknown God: Negative Theology in the Platonic Tradition: Plato to Eriugena* (Louvain: Peeters Press, Eerdmans, 1995), 241.

6. Pseudo-Dionysius, *Divine Names,* 49–50.

7. Janet Williams, "The Apophatic Theology of Dionysius the Pseudo-Areopagite — I," *Downside Review* 117 (July 1999): 165.

8. Aquinas, *Summa,* I.I Question 12, Article 7, 101.

9. Ibid., Article 1, 92.

10. Karl Rahner, "The Hiddenness of God," *Theological Investigations,* vol. 16, trans. David Morland (New York: Seabury Press, 1979), 229.

11. Interview with Karl-Heinz Weger for Radio Austria, Vienna, March 2, 1979 as transcribed in *Karl Rahner in Dialogue,* ed. Paul Imhof and Hubert Biallowons, trans. ed. Harvey D. Egan (New York: Crossroad, 1986), 211.

12. Karl Rahner, *Foundations of Christian Faith: An Introduction to the Idea of Christianity,* trans. William V. Dych (New York: Crossroad, 1978), 64.

13. Aquinas, *Summa Contra Gentiles,* chapter LXII, Pegis, vol. 2:110.

14. Karl Rahner, "An Investigation of the Incomprehensibility of God in St. Thomas Aquinas," *Theological Investigations,* 16:246.

15. Teresa of Avila, "Spiritual Testimonies," in *The Collected Works of St. Teresa of Avila,* trans. Kieran Kavanaugh and Otilio Rodriguez (Washington, D.C.: ICS Publications Institute of Carmelite Studies, 1976), 328.

16. Joseph A. Fitzmyer, *The Anchor Bible: Acts of the Apostles, New Translation with Introduction and Commentary* (New York: Doubleday: 1998), 302.

17. Karl Barth, *Church Dogmatics*, vol. 2, ed. G. W. Bromiley and T. F. Torrance (Edinburgh: T & T Clark, 1957), 56.

18. Ibid., 4.

Chapter Two / Historical Resources

1. Elisabeth Schüssler Fiorenza, *In Memory of Her: A Feminist Theological Reconstruction of Christian Origins* (New York: Crossroad, 1992), xvii.

2. Homi K. Bhabha, *The Location of Culture* (London and New York: Routledge, 1994).

3. Alan F. Segal, *Rebecca's Children: Judaism and Christianity in the Roman World* (Cambridge, Mass.: Harvard University Press, 1986), 148–50.

4. Clement of Alexandria, Miscellanies 1.25, in *The Ante-Nicene Fathers: Translations of the Fathers down to A.D. 325*, vol. 2, *Fathers of the Second Century*, ed. Alexander Roberts and James Donaldson (Grand Rapids, Mich.: Eerdmans, 1981), 316, as quoted in Dale T. Irvin and Scott W. Sunquist, *History of the World Christian Movement*, vol. 1: *Earliest Christianity to 1453* (Maryknoll, N.Y.: Orbis, 2001), 86 and 122–24. See also Samuel Hugh Moffett, *A History of Christianity in Asia*, vol. 1: *Beginnings to 1500*, 2nd revised and corrected ed. (Maryknoll, N.Y.: Orbis, 1998), 38.

5. *The Acts of Judas Thomas*, trans. A. F. J. Klijn (Leiden: E. J. Brill, 1962). Many Christians in India trace their heritage to the Apostle Thomas and there are early written sources that reference this legend, for example Eusebius (second century) and John Chrysostom (fourth century). See Stephen Neill, *A History of Christianity in India, The Beginnings to AD 1707* (Cambridge: Cambridge University Press, 1984), 26–48. For a discussion of earliest Christian presence in India see, Samuel Hugh Moffett, *A History of Christianity in Asia, Volume I: Beginnings to 1500*, 2nd rev.and corrected edition (Maryknoll, N.Y.: Orbis, 1998), 24–38.

6. *The Acts of Judas Thomas*, Act 2.19, Klijn p. 74.

7. Ibid., Act 2.21, Klijn pp. 74–75.

8. Ibid., Act 2.19, Klijn p. 74.

9. Jon Sobrino, *Christ the Liberator: A View from the Victims*, trans. Paul Burns (Maryknoll, N.Y.: Orbis, 2001), 248.

10. "The Martyrdom of Saints Perpetua and Felicitas" in *Acts of the Christian Martyrs* (Oxford: Clarendon Press, 1972), 113.

11. Cyprian of Carthage, *Epistle* 4, 4 (Corpus Scriptorum Ecclesiastico-rum Latinorum), cited in Jacques Dupuis, *Toward a Christian Theology of Religious Pluralism* (Maryknoll, N.Y.: Orbis, 1997), 88.

12. Francis Sullivan, *Salvation outside the Church? Tracing the History of the Catholic Response* (New York: Paulist Press, 1992), 5–6.

13. Sobrino, *Christ the Liberator,* 237.

14. Bartolomé de Las Casas, *The Devastation of the Indies: A Brief Account,* trans. Herma Briffault (Baltimore: Johns Hopkins University Press, 1992), 33–34.

15. Ibid., 44.

16. Ibid., 45.

17. Michael Wood, *Conquistadors* (Berkeley and Los Angeles: University of California Press, 2000), 141.

18. Francis Xavier, *The Letters and Instructions of Francis Xavier,* trans. M. Joseph Costelloe (St. Louis: Institute of Jesuit Sources, 1992), 48.

19. *Epistolae Xaverianae,* 1:148. Quoted in Stephen Neill, *History of Christianity in India,* 143.

20. Xavier, letter dated January 15, 1544, *The Letters and Instructions of Francis Xavier,* 66.

21. De Nobili, "Customs of the Indian Nation," in *Preaching Wisdom to the Wise: Three Treatises by Roberto de Nobili, S.J., Missionary and Scholar in Seventeenth-Century India,* trans. Anand Amaladass and Francis X. Clooney (St. Louis: Institute of Jesuit Sources, 2000), 221.

22. Neill, *History of Christianity in India,* 281.

23. Vincent Cronin, *A Pearl to India: The Life of Roberto de Nobili* (London: Rupert Hart-Davis, 1959), 46–47.

24. Roberto de Nobili, "Dialogue on Eternal Life," in *Preaching Wisdom to the Wise,* 244.

25. Ibid., 262.

26. de Nobili to Laerzio, February 20, 1609, quoted in Cronin, *A Pearl to India,* 99.

27. Robert McClory, *Faithful Dissenters: Stories of Men and Women Who Loved and Changed the Church* (Maryknoll, N.Y.: Orbis, 2000), 92.

28. Matteo Ricci, *The True Meaning of the Lord of Heaven (T'ien-chu Shih-i),* trans. Douglas Lancashire and Peter Hu Kuo-chen, Chinese-English edition ed. Edward J. Malatesta (St. Louis: Institute of Jesuit Sources and Taipei: Ricci Institute for Chinese Studies, 1985), 71.

29. Ibid., 61.

30. Ibid., 125.

31. Lancashire and Kuo-chen, "Translators' Introduction," in Matteo Ricci, *The True Meaning of the Lord of Heaven,* 46.

32. Adrian Hastings, "Were Women a Special Case?" in *Women and Missions: Past and Present, Anthropological and Historical Perceptions,*

ed. Fiona Bowie, Deborah Kirkwood, and Shirley Ardener (Providence, R.I., and Oxford: Berg Publishers, 1993), 115.

33. Ibid. See also, Steven Kaplan, "The Africanization of Missionary Christianity," in *Indigenous Responses to Western Christianity*, ed. Steven Kaplan (New York: New York University Press, 1995), 9–28; *Christianity in Africa as Seen by Africans*, ed. Ram Desai (Denver: Alan Swallow, 1962).

34. David Chidester, *Savage Systems: Colonialism and Comparative Religion in Southern Africa* (Charlottesville: University Press of Virginia, 1996), 9.

35. See, e.g., Torben Christensen and William R. Hutchison, eds., *Missionary Ideologies in the Imperialist Era: 1880–1920* (Arhus, Denmark: Aros Publishers, 1982); Sara H. Sohmer, "Christianity Without Civilization," *Journal of Religious History* 18, no. 2 (December 1994): 174–97. For a critique of this same "civilizing" mission in early anthropologies see, Trinh T. Minh-ha, *Woman Native Other: Writing Postcoloniality and Feminism* (Bloomington and Indianapolis: Indiana University Press, 1989); Jose Rabasa, "Dialogue as Conquest: Mapping Spaces for Counter-Discourse," in *The Nature and Context of Minority Discourse*, ed. Abdul R. JanMohamed and David Lloyd (Oxford: Oxford University Press, 1990), 187–215; Edward Said, "Representing the Colonized: Anthropology's Interlocutors," *Critical Inquiry* 15, no. 1 (1989): 205–25.

36. Andrew Barnes, "Evangelization Where it is Not Wanted: Colonial Administrators and Missionaries in Northern Nigeria During the First Third of the Twentieth Century," *Journal of Religion in Africa* 25, no. 4 (1995): 412ff.

37. Jean Woolmington, "Missionary Attitudes to the Baptism of Australian Aborigines before 1850," *Journal of Religious History* 13 (June 1985): 283–93.

38. John Hick, "The Non-Absoluteness of Christianity," in *The Myth of Christian Uniqueness*, ed. John Hick and Paul Knitter (Maryknoll, N.Y.: Orbis, 1987), 19–20.

39. *The Missionary Register*, Church Missionary Society, September 1818, 374–75, as cited in Homi K. Bhabha, "Sly Civility," in *The Location of Culture*, 99.

Chapter Three / The Impasse of Sameness or Difference

1. Karl Barth, *Church Dogmatics*, vol. 2: *The Doctrine of God*, ed. G. W. Bromiley and T. F. Torrance (Edinburgh: T & T Clark, 1957), 45.

2. Ibid., 2: 180.

3. Barth, "The Revelation of God as the Abolition of Religion," *Church Dogmatics*. vol. 1, chap. 2: *The Revelation of God*, ed. G. W. Bromiley and T. F. Torrance (New York: Charles Scribner's Sons, 1956), 280–361.

4. Roger Haight, *Jesus Symbol of God* (Maryknoll, N.Y.: Orbis, 1999), 404.

5. Congregation for the Doctrine of the Faith, "Declaration: *Dominus Iesus* on the Unicity and Salvific Universality of Jesus Christ and the Church," §6. Online at www.vatican.va/roman_curia/congregations/cfaith/documents/rc_con_cfaith_doc_20000806_dominus-iesus_en.html.

6. *Dominus Iesus,* §22.

7. Diana Eck, *A New Religious America: How a "Christian Country" Has Become the World's Most Religiously Diverse Nation* (New York: HarperCollins, 2001), 309.

8. *Dominus Iesus,* §12.

9. Ibid., §2.

10. Karl Rahner, *Foundations of Christian Faith: An Introduction to the Idea of Christianity,* trans. William V. Dych (New York: Crossroad, 1978), 139.

11. George Vass, *Understanding Karl Rahner,* vol. 3: *A Pattern of Christian Doctrines* (London: Sheed & Ward, 1985), 44. "Strictly speaking, this latter dimension of God's reality [i.e., God's self-communication] is the one which lets his presence not only be known but be experienced by man [sic], his creation."

12. Karl Rahner, *On Prayer* (New York: Paulist Press, 1968), 25.

13. Rahner, *Foundations,* 143.

14. Ibid., 153.

15. Ibid., 211.

16. Ibid., 170.

17. Karl Rahner, "The One Christ and the Universality of Salvation," *Theological Investigations,* vol. 16, trans. David Morland (New York: Seabury Press, 1979), 200.

18. Karl Rahner, "Christianity and the Non-Christian Religions," *Theological Investigations,* vol. 5, trans. Karl-H. Kruger (Baltimore: Helicon Press, 1966), 118.

19. Rahner, *Foundations,* 147.

20. Karl Rahner, "Anonymous Christians," *Theological Investigations,* vol. 6, trans. Karl-H. Kruger and Boniface Kruger (New York: Seabury Press, 1974), 395.

21. Jacques Dupuis, *Toward a Christian Theology of Religious Pluralism* (Maryknoll, N.Y.: Orbis, 1997), 387.

22. The distinction between inclusivism and the exclusivist leanings in the official documents of the Catholic Church are illuminated in the response Dupuis has received from Rome. The Congregation for the Doctrine of the Faith completed an investigation of Dupuis's work and pronounced that his work compromised central doctrinal principles. Articulated as

binding on Catholic Christians is the principle that "Jesus Christ, the son of God made man, crucified and risen, is the sole mediator of salvation for all humanity." Furthermore, "it is contrary to the Catholic faith to consider other religions as 'complementary ways' of salvation; the followers of other religions are 'oriented to the church and are called to be part of her.'" Cited in *America,* March 12, 2001, 5.

23. Gavin D'Costa, "Christ, the Trinity and Religious Pluralism," in *Christian Uniqueness Reconsidered: The Myth of a Pluralistic Theology of Religions,* ed. Gavin D'Costa (Maryknoll, N.Y.: Orbis, 1990), 17.

24. See, e.g., *The Trinity in a Pluralistic Age: Theological Essays on Culture and Religion,* ed. Kevin J. Vanhoozer (Grand Rapids, Mich.: Eerdmans, 1997).

25. John Cobb, *Christ in a Pluralistic Age* (Philadelphia: Westminster, 1975).

26. Raimundo Panikkar, *The Unknown Christ of Hinduism: Toward an Ecumenical Christophany,* rev. and enl. ed. (London: Darton, Longman & Todd, 1981).

27. For a discussion of the nuance at the border between inclusivist and pluralist thinking see Maurice Wiles, "The Meaning of Christ," in *God, Truth and Reality: Essays in Honour of John Hick,* ed. Arvind Sharma (New York: St. Martin's Press, 1993), 221–35.

28. Roberto de Nobili, "Dialogue on Eternal Life" in *Preaching Wisdom to the Wise: Three Treatises by Roberto de Nobili, S.J., Missionary and Scholar in 17th Century India,* trans. Anand Amaladass and Francis X. Clooney (St. Louis: Institute of Jesuit Sources, 2000), 262.

29. *The Missionary Register,* Church Missionary Society, September 1818, 374–75, as cited in Homi K. Bhabha, "Sly Civility," in *The Location of Culture,* 99.

30. John Hick, *A Christian Theology of Religions: The Rainbow of Faiths* (Louisville: Westminster John Knox, 1995), 27.

31. Ibid., 107.

32. Ibid., 77–78.

33. S. Mark Heim, *Salvations: Truth and Difference in Religion* (Maryknoll, N.Y.: Orbis, 1995), 110.

34. Anne M. Blackburn, "Magic in the Monastery: Textual Practice and Monastic Identity in Sri Lanka" *History of Religions* 38, no. 4 (1999): 354.

35. Helene Stork, "Mothering Rituals in Tamilnadu: Some Magico-Religious Beliefs," in *Roles and Rituals for Hindu Women,* ed. Julia Leslie (Delhi: Motilal Banarsidass Publishers, 1992), 101.

36. G. Saraswathi, "Agamic Way of Worshipping God and Priesthood in Three Different Temples of Mysore District," *Man in India* 79, nos. 1–2 (1999): 94–95.

37. Anna Portnoy, "There in the Making: In Search of an AIDS Goddess," thesis presented to the Committee on the Study of Religion, Harvard College, March 2000.

38. Frederick M. Smith, "Indra Goes West: Report on a Vedic Soma Sacrifice in London in July 1996," *History of Religions* 39, no. 3 (2000): 247–67.

39. Qur'an 2:45–63;4:153–176;5;9:16–40;43:57–64;57:26–29.

40. George Lindbeck, *The Nature of Doctrine: Religion and Theology in a Postliberal Age* (Philadelphia: Westminster, 1984), 33.

41. Ibid., 34.

42. Thomas Kuhn, *The Structure of Scientific Revolutions*, 2nd ed. (Chicago: University of Chicago Press, 1970), 113.

43. Lindbeck, *"Fides ex Auditu* and the Salvation of Non-Christians: Contemporary Catholic and Protestant Positions," in *The Gospel and the Ambiguity of the Church,* ed. Vilmos Vajta (Philadelphia: Fortress Press, 1974), 119.

44. Lindbeck, *"Fides ex Auditu,"* 119.

45. Lindbeck, "The Story-Shaped Church: Critical Exegesis and Theological Interpretation," in *Scriptural Authority and Narrative Interpretation,* ed. Garrett Green (Philadelphia: Fortress Press, 1987), 161–78.

46. Lindbeck draws on the work of Ronald Thiemann in describing the text in this way. See Lindbeck's "Scripture, Consensus and Community," 96; and Thiemann's "Radiance and Obscurity in Biblical Narrative" in *Scriptural Authority and Narrative Interpretation,* 21–41.

47. George Lindbeck, "The Framework of Protestant-Catholic Disagreement," in *The Word in History: The St. Xavier Symposium,* ed. T. Patrick Burke (New York: Sheed and Ward, 1966), 117.

48. George Lindbeck, "The Future of Dialogue: Pluralism or an Eventual Synthesis of Doctrine," in *Christian Action and Openness to the World,* ed. Joseph Papin (Villanova, Pa.: Villanova University Press, 1970), 46.

49. Lindbeck, *Nature of Doctrine,* 22.

50. George Lindbeck, "The Gospel's Uniqueness: Election and Untranslatability," *Modern Theology* 13, no. 4 (October 1997): 423.

51. Lindbeck, *Nature of Doctrine,* 41.

52. Ibid., 40.

53. Lindbeck, "The Gospel's Uniqueness," 427.

54. S. Mark Heim, *Salvations: Truth and Difference in Religion* (Maryknoll, N.Y.: Orbis, 1995), 227.

55. Lindbeck, *Nature of Doctrine,* 23.

56. Russell T. McCutcheon, "The Imperial Dynamic in the Study of Religion: Neocolonial Practices in an American Discipline," in *Postcolonial America,* ed. C. Richard King (Urbana and Chicago: University of Illinois Press, 2000), 298.

57. Hick, *Christian Theology of Religion*, 30.

58. S. Mark Heim, *The Depth of The Riches: A Trinitarian Theology of Religious Ends* (Grand Rapids, Mich.: Eerdmans, 2001), 17–49; Heim, "Saving the Particulars: Religious Experience and Religious Ends," *Religious Studies* 36 (2000): 435–53.

Chapter Four / We Are All Hybrids

1. Francis Schüssler Fiorenza, *Foundational Theology: Jesus and the Church* (New York: Crossroad, 1992), 215.

2. Harvey Cox, "Christianity" in *Our Religions,* ed. Arvind Sharma (New York: HarperSanFrancisco, 1993), 360.

3. Iris Marion Young, "The Ideal Community and the Politics of Difference" in *Feminism/Postmodernism,* ed. Linda J. Nicholson (New York: Routledge, 1990), 303. Originally in *Social Theory and Practice* 12, no. 1 (Spring 1986): 1–26.

4. George Lindbeck, "The Future of Dialogue: Pluralism or an Eventual Synthesis of Doctrine," in *Christian Action and Openness to the World,* ed. Joseph Papin (Villanova, Pa.: Villanova University Press, 1970), 45–46.

5. Karl Rahner, "Ecumenical Togetherness Today," *Theological Investigations,* vol. 22, trans. Joseph Donceel (New York: Crossroad, 1991), 93; and "Ecumenical Theology in the Future," *Theological Investigations,* vol. 14, trans. David Bourke (New York: Seabury Press, 1976), 255–56.

6. Jean Grimshaw, *Philosophy and Feminist Thinking* (Minneapolis: University of Minnesota Press, 1986), 85.

7. Elizabeth V. Spelman, *Inessential Woman: Problems of Exclusion in Feminist Thought* (Boston: Beacon Press, 1988), 137.

8. Chung Hyun Kyung, *Struggle to be the Sun Again: Introducing Asian Women's Theology* (Maryknoll, N.Y.: Orbis, 1990).

9. Morwenna Griffiths, *Feminisms and the Self: The Web of Identity* (London and New York: Routledge, 1995), 2.

10. Ibid, 182.

11. Martha Minnow, *Not Only for Myself* (New York: New Press, 1997), 40.

12. Carol P. Christ and Judith Plaskow, eds., *Womanspirit Rising: A Feminist Reader in Religion* (San Francisco: Harper & Row, 1979).

13. Judith Plaskow and Carol P. Christ, eds., *Weaving the Visions: New Patterns in Feminist Spirituality* (San Francisco: HarperSanFrancisco, 1989).

14. Paula M. Cooey, William R. Eakin, Jay B. McDaniel, eds., *After Patriarchy: Feminist Transformations of the World Religions* (Maryknoll, N.Y.: Orbis, 1991).

15. Carol P. Christ, "Roundtable: Feminist Theology and Religious Diversity," *Journal of Feminist Studies in Religion* 16, no. 2 (2000): 79.

16. Rita Gross, "Feminist Theology as Theology of Religions," in *The Cambridge Companion to Feminist Theology*, ed. Susan Frank Parsons (Cambridge: Cambridge University Press, 2002), 68. In valuing the otherness that we encounter in the "comparative mirror," it is important to avoid replicating colonialist encounters where otherness is primarily valued for how it can serve one's own aims. In each encounter, we must be keenly aware of the power differentials that structure the gaze across the comparative mirror, placing in primacy the goals of justice. See Kwok Pui-lan, in the Introduction to *Postcolonialism, Feminism and Religious Discourse*, ed. Laura E. Donaldson and Kwok Pui-lan (New York and London: Routledge, 2002), 26–28.

17. Iain Chambers, "Signs of Silence, Lines of Listening," in *The Post-Colonial Question: Common Skies, Divided Horizons*, ed. Iain Chambers and Lidia Curti (London and New York: Routledge, 1996), 54.

18. Ann Ferguson, "A Feminist Aspect Theory of the Self," in *Women, Knowledge and Reality: Explorations in Feminist Philosophy*, ed. Ann Garry and Marilyn Pearsall (New York and London: Routledge, 1992), 93–107. Reprinted from *Science, Morality and Feminist Theory*, ed. Marsha Hanen and Kai Nielsen, *Canadian Journal of Philosophy*, supplementary vol. 13 (1988): 339–56.

19. John Tomlinson, "The Possibility of Cosmopolitanism," in *Globalization and Culture* (Chicago: University of Chicago Press, 1999), 206.

20. Jane Flax envisions the various dimensions of identity, including gender, as verbs. See her *Disputed Subjects: Essays on Psychoanalysis, Politics and Philosophy* (New York and London: Routledge, 1993), 23.

21. Griffiths, *Feminisms and the Self*, 92.

22. Nancy Julia Chodrow, "Gender, Relation, and Difference in Psychoanalytic Perspective," in *Feminist Social Thought*, ed. Diana Tietjens Meyers (New York and London: Routledge, 1997), 11. Reprinted from *Socialist Review* 9, no. 46 (1979): 51–69.

23. For other examples of African encounter with Christian forms see, Steven Kaplan, "The Africanization of Missionary Christianity," in *Indigenous Responses to Western Christianity*, ed. Steven Kaplan (New York: New York University Press, 1995), 9–28; and *Christianity in Africa as Seen by Africans*, ed. Ram Desai (Denver: Alan Swallow, 1962).

24. Birgit Meyer, "Beyond Syncretism: Translation and Diabolization in the Appropriation of Protestantism in Africa," in *Syncretism/Anti-Syncretism*, 45–68; Robert J. Schreiter, *Constructing Local Theologies* (Maryknoll, N.Y.: Orbis, 1985), 146; Eugene D. Genovese, *Roll, Jordan, Roll: The World the Slaves Made* (New York: Vintage Books, 1976).

25. Cristián Parker Gumucio, "Chile: Identity and Diversity in Urban Popular Catholicism," in *Popular Catholicism in a World Church*, ed. Thomas Bamat and Jean-Paul Wiest (Maryknoll, N.Y.: Orbis, 1999), 30.

26. David Mosse, "Catholic Saints and the Hindu Village Pantheon in Rural Tamil Nadu, India," *Man* 12, no. 1–2 (1994): 301–32.

27. Panikkar is the author of numerous theological works at the intersection of Hinduism and Christianity, notably *The Unknown Christ of Hinduism: Toward an Ecumenical Christophany* (London: Darton, Longman & Todd, 1964). For a discussion of his shaping by multiple traditions, see his, "Religious Identity and Pluralism," in *Dome of Many Colors: Studies in Religious Pluralism, Identity and Unity*, ed. Arvind Sharma and Kathleen M. Dugan (Harrisburg, Pa.: Trinity Press International, 1999), 23–47.

28. Bhabha, "Signs Taken for Wonders," in *The Location of Culture* (London and New York: Routledge, 1994), 116.

29. A consideration of religions as unbounded categories comes from Benson Saler's *Conceptualizing Religion: Immanent Anthropologists, Transcendent Natives, and Unbounded Categories* (London and New York: E. J. Brill, 1993), 254ff.

30. Trinh T. Minh-ha, *Woman-Native-Other* (Bloomington and Indianapolis: Indiana University Press, 1989), 93–94.

31. Francis X. Clooney, "The Study of Non-Christian Religions in the Post-Vatican II Roman Catholic Church," *Journal of Ecumenical Studies* 28, no. 3 (Summer 1991): 489.

Chapter Five / Living Religious Pluralism

1. Gordon D. Kaufman, *In Face of Mystery: A Constructive Theology* (Cambridge, Mass.: Harvard University Press, 1993), 317.

2. George Lindbeck, "Scripture, Consensus and Community," in *Biblical Interpretation in Crisis: The Ratzinger Conference on Bible and Church*, ed. Richard John Neuhaus (Grand Rapids, Mich.: Eerdmans, 1989), 95.

3. George Lindbeck, "The Story-Shaped Church: Critical Exegesis and Theological Interpretation," in *Scriptural Authority and Narrative Interpretation*, ed. Garrett Green (Philadelphia: Fortress Press, 1987), 165–70.

4. George Lindbeck, "The Gospel's Uniqueness: Election and Untranslatability," *Modern Theology* 13, no. 4 (October 1997): 432.

5. This echoes the concept of intersectional membership articulated by Martha Minnow, *Not Only for Myself: Identity, Politics, and the Law* (New York: New Press, 1997), 50.

6. Michael Amaladoss, *Life in Freedom: Liberation Theologies from Asia* (Maryknoll, N.Y.: Orbis, 1997), 132.

7. Ibid., 132–33.

8. Elisabeth Schüssler Fiorenza, *In Memory of Her: A Feminist Theological Reconstruction of Christian Origins* (New York: Crossroad, 1992), 123.

9. Marcus Borg, "From Galilean Jew to Face of God," in *Jesus at 2000*, ed. Marcus Borg (Boulder, Colo.: Westview Press, 1997), 11.

10. Schüssler Fiorenza, *In Memory of Her*, 120.

11. Ibid., 105–54.

12. Borg, "From Galilean Jew to Face of God," 11.

13. Elisabeth Schüssler Fiorenza, *Jesus: Miriam's Child, Sophia's Prophet* (New York: Continuum, 1995), 157.

14. Walter Rauschenbusch, *Theology for the Social Gospel* (New York: Macmillan, 1917), 248–63.

15. Jon Sobrino, *Christ the Liberator* (Maryknoll, N.Y.: Orbis, 2001), 217.

16. Ibid., 83–84.

17. Schüssler Fiorenza, *Jesus: Miriam's Child, Sophia's Prophet*, 137.

18. Joseph A. Fitzmyer, *The Anchor Bible: Acts of the Apostles, New Translation with Introduction and Commentary* (New York: Doubleday: 1998), 302.

19. Roger Haight, *Jesus, Symbol of God* (Maryknoll, N.Y.: Orbis, 1999), 167.

20. Francis Schüssler Fiorenza, *Foundational Theology: Jesus and the Church* (New York: Crossroad, 1992), 133.

21. Luke Timothy Johnson, *The Anchor Bible: First and Second Letters to Timothy, A New Translation with Introduction and Commentary* (New York: Doubleday, 2001), 197.

22. Ibid., 191.

23. Gustavo Gutiérrez, *A Theology of Liberation: History Politics and Salvation*, rev. ed., trans. and ed. Caridad Inda and John Eagleson (Maryknoll, N.Y.: Orbis, 1988), 85. Gutiérrez goes on to see the transformation of the world as leading to a fullness in Christ. The Christological aspect is one way in which to identify a powerful form of liberation and salvation, but as this text has argued, such Christological focus need not rule out other forms of liberation/salvation.

24. See, e.g., Paul Knitter, *One Earth Many Religions: Multifaith Dialogue and Global Responsibility* (Maryknoll, N.Y.: Orbis, 1995), 113.

25. Ada María Isasi-Díaz, "Solidarity: Love of Neighbor in the Twenty-First Century," in *Mujerista Theology: A Theology for the Twenty-First Century* (Maryknoll, N.Y.: Orbis, 1996), 89.

26. Maurice Wiles, *Christian Theology and Inter-religious Dialogue* (London: SCM Press; Philadelphia: Trinity Press International, 1992), 74

27. Elisabeth Schüssler Fiorenza, *Bread Not Stone: The Challenge of Feminist Biblical Interpretation* (Boston: Beacon Press, 1995), 32.

28. Ibid., 35.

29. Luke Timothy Johnson, *The Gospel of Luke*, Sacra Pagina Series 3, ed. Daniel J. Harrington (Collegeville, Minn.: Liturgical Press), 109.

30. *The New Jerome Biblical Commentary,* ed. Raymond Brown, Joseph Fitzmyer, Roland Murphy (Englewood Cliffs, N.J.: Prentice Hall, 1990), 695.

31. Paul Tillich, *Dynamics of Faith* (New York: Harper & Brothers, 1958), 2–3.

32. R. J. Coggins, *Samaritans and Jews: The Origins of Samaritanism Reconsidered* (Oxford: Basil Blackwell, 1975).

33. See S. Mark Heim, *The Depth of The Riches: A Trinitarian Theology of Religious Ends* (Grand Rapids, Mich.: Eerdmans, 2001), 17–49; Heim, "Saving the Particulars: Religious Experience and Religious Ends," *Religious Studies* 36 (2000): 435–53.

34. Karl Rahner, "The Hiddenness of God," *Theological Investigations,* vol. 16, trans. David Morland (New York: Seabury Press, 1979), 229.

35. Karl Rahner, "An Investigation of the Incomprehensibility of God in St. Thomas Aquinas," *Theological Investigations,* 16:247.

36. Karl Rahner, "Being Open to God as Ever Greater," *Theological Investigations,* vol. 7, trans. David Bourke (New York: Seabury Press, 1977), 44.

37. Rita Gross, "Feminist Theology as Theology of Religions," in *The Cambridge Companion to Feminist Theology,* ed. Susan Frank Parsons (Cambridge: Cambridge University Press, 2002), 68.

38. Karl Rahner, *Foundations of Christian Faith: An Introduction to the Idea of Christianity,* trans. William V. Dych (New York: Crossroad, 1978), 127.

39. Karl Rahner, "The Concept of Mystery in Catholic Theology," *Theological Investigations,* vol. 4, trans. Kevin Smyth (London: Darton, Longman & Todd, 1966), 62.

40. Ibid., 62.

41. Karl Rahner, "An Investigation of the Incomprehensibility of God in St. Thomas Aquinas," *Theological Investigations,* 16:246.

INDEX